Making Room in Our Hearts

"Every once in a while, a book comes along that can make an honest difference in the understanding of an important subject—and, therefore, in people's lives. I'm delighted to say that **Making Room in Our Hearts** is one of those books. It takes on open adoption, which remains too poorly understood despite its growing prevalence, and explains it in the best possible way: through the stories of those who live it. The result is simultaneously touching and enlightening; it's a wonderful combination that I hope and believe will make an honest difference in the continued evolution of adoption from the stigmatized, secretive process that it used to be into one that is honest, healthy and better serves all of its participants, especially the children."

— Adam Pertman, executive director, Evan B. Donaldson Adoption Institute

"Micky Duxbury has written an interesting, up-to-date book on the beauty and the complexity of families built through open adoption. She has integrated the knowledge provided by other experts in the field with the poignant sharings of real families who have been living their open adoptions over several years. This is a book well worth reading and owning; I highly recommend it."

— Sharon Roszia, co-author of *The Open Adoption Experience* and program manager, Special Needs Adoptions for Kinship Center of Southern California

"Open adoption is not a trend—it is the wave of the future. **Making Room in Our Hearts** helps us prepare for that future by providing an ethical and child-centered perspective as it puts a human face on open adoption. You will meet real people revealing, as well as struggling with the ups and downs of these complex relationships. This book fills an important need by providing adoption professionals, birth and adoptive families and their extended familial networks with a wealth of practical and personal information."

— Brenda Romanchik, MSW, open adoption educator, birth parent advocate, and director of Insight: Open Adoption Resources and Support

"Having been born under the closed adoption system some forty-something years ago, it was a profoundly moving experience for me to read about families—birth and adoptive families—who have come to embrace openness for their children. I believe that the adoption community is moving in a brave and important new direction, and that Micky Duxbury's book will provide a vital map for families and professionals alike. I am grateful for this work and only wish that it had been the standard of practice while I was growing up."

— Susan Ito, adult adoptee and co-editor of *A Ghost At Heart's Edge: Stories & Poems of Adoption*

"**Making Room in Our Hearts** is an authentic, inside account of the open adoption experience. It offers an opportunity to listen in as the participants of adoption describe the delights and challenges of their journeys. Openness never shines brighter than when it is expressed in the actual words of those who live it day in and day out."

— James Gritter, author of *The Spirit of Open Adoption*, and *The Lifegivers: Framing the Birth Parent Experience in Adoption*

"This is a wonderful book … and the author seems to have complete control of this often-confusing area of relationships. The topic is covered in a thorough as well as realistic fashion. Duxbury is a skilled writer and has a very friendly writing style that should appeal to the reader …. As families become more and more 'non-traditional,' the notion of openness cannot be stressed enough."

— Jon Carlson, Psy.D., Ed.D., ABPP, distinguished professor, Governors State University

"I have been anxiously awaiting the release of **Making Room in Our Hearts**, by Micky Duxbury so that I could recommend it to every adopting family I have the fortune of consulting with. Never has there been a volume so compassionate, inspiring and informative about why child-centered open adoption is the correct paradigm for today's adoptions. Ms. Duxbury understands that openness in adoption is not a quantifiable obligation, but a quality that can be cultivated and reside in the heart of family members touched by adoption."

— Leslie Foge, MA, MFT, adoption psychotherapist and co-author of *The Third Choice: A Woman's Guide for Placing a Child for Adoption*

"This book is a valuable inclusion as an educational tool in the arena of open adoption … that can build understanding among those personally involved with adoption, considering adoption, professionals and anyone else who is interested in this topic. Additionally, it offers support to those already in open adoptions who want to hear about how this experience has evolved for others as the years have passed."

— Patricia Martinez Dorner, MA, LPC, LMFT, co-author of *Children of Open Adoption* and author of *How to Open an Adoption: A Guide for Parents and Birthparents of Minors*

Making Room in Our Hearts

Keeping Family Ties through Open Adoption

Micky Duxbury

Routledge
Taylor & Francis Group
New York   London

Routledge is an imprint of the
Taylor & Francis Group, an informa business

Routledge
Taylor & Francis Group
711 Third Avenue
New York, NY 10017

Routledge
Taylor & Francis Group
2 Park Square
Milton Park, Abingdon
Oxon OX14 4RN

© 2007 by Micky Duxbury
Routledge is an imprint of Taylor & Francis Group, an Informa business

International Standard Book Number-10: 0-415-95502-5 (Softcover)
International Standard Book Number-13: 978-0-415-95502-7 (Softcover)

Library of Congress Cataloging-in-Publication Data

Duxbury, Micky, 1948-
  Making room in our hearts : keeping family ties through open adoption / Micky Duxbury.
     p. cm.
  Includes bibliographical references.
  ISBN 0-415-95502-5 (pb : alk. paper)
    1. Open adoption--United States--Case studies. I. Title.

HV875.55.D89 2007
362.734--dc22   2006014125

Visit the Taylor & Francis Web site at
http://www.taylorandfrancis.com

and the Routledge Web site at
http://www.routledge-ny.com

To my daughter
Loving you has been one of the greatest blessings of my life

To her birth parents
You created a beautiful child who is passionate about life

and

To my mother, Mildred Duxbury, who taught me about
the sacred ties between mother and daughter

Contents

Foreword

I was born under the closed adoption system over four decades ago, and it moved me deeply to read about contemporary families—birth and adoptive families who have come to embrace openness for their children. When I was growing up, thoughts of my birth family were as abstract as the way I thought of movie stars or fairies. They were not real people to me, and since I had come from them, that lack of basic information made me feel a little less real than nonadopted people. I cannot even imagine what it would have been like to be able to point to a photo, or to speak a name out loud and say, "They are my birth parents." Instead, they were secret people, whose names were not known, let alone mentioned, and whose faces were perpetually in shadow.

Closed adoptions were justified as a means of protecting the birth mother, and in those days of shame and "illegitimacy" they may have served that purpose. But under that protective layer of anonymity, there was also unspeakable pain and loss, and an endless sense of unknowing for all parties. Open adoptions today are undeniably complex and result in ever-evolving relationships that may not be as "easy" as the secrecy of the past. However, I believe that they are infinitely healthier for everyone involved; not just for adoptees, but also for birth and adoptive parents, each of whom suffered under the weight of not knowing in the closed system. I grew up believing that I was someone else's darkest, most awful secret, and the shame of my out-of-wedlock birth cast a shadow on my life. I had no idea of who my birth family might be, much less where they might be found, and I could not answer the most basic of question about my ethnicity: what are you?

As some of the situations in this book illustrate, the truth can indeed be hard to deal with, but I believe that even a difficult truth is ultimately better than deception or secrecy. The families whose stories appear in this book make it clear that openness is not a panacea; it does not and cannot ease all of the psychological and spiritual struggles that adoptees experience as they build their own identities. But building an identity based on knowing who you are and where you come from is a very different task from building one based on fantasy and a few meager details doled out from a file of non-identifying information.

The families who chose to share their stories and varied experiences in this book have given authentic voices to the concept of open adoption. Their honesty in sharing both their struggles and joys is touching and inspiring. They tell us that it can be done, and that for the majority, it is more than worth the challenge. I believe that the adoption community is moving in a brave and important new direction, and that *Making Room in Our Hearts* will provide guidance and support for families and professionals alike. I am grateful for this work and only wish that open adoption had been the standard of practice while I was growing up. It is certainly the best possible practice for the future.

Susan Ito

Adult adoptee and co-editor of *A Ghost at Heart's Edge:
Stories and Poems of Adoption*

Introduction

Over the past ten years, I have been observing some of the open adoption landscape as an adoption educator and therapist, and as an adoptive parent. As a leader of adoption support groups for the Northern California Chapter of Resolve, I have worked with many couples and individuals as they have struggled with their concerns about open adoption. For adoptive parents, considering ongoing relationships with birth parents often feels like a threat to their yet-to-be established parenting. For women and men facing the reality of unplanned pregnancies, the idea of developing a relationship with the adoptive family is often seen as new and potentially risky territory. They have questions about their rights to continued contact, how changes will be negotiated, and what kind of relationship they will be able to have with their child in the future.

In spite of their mutual fears and concerns, these families move forward when they are able to understand the benefits of openness for the child. Hearing from families already in open relationships and listening to the experience of adopted persons are vital ingredients in this process. Choosing adoption professionals who support a child-centered approach to open adoption is also an important ingredient, but for many professionals in the adoption community, openness is still a take-it-or-leave-it proposition. Birth and adoptive parents may be encouraged to meet during the matching process and exchange occasional letters and photos, but few are educated about how families negotiate these complex relationships over time.

Over 150 birth or adoptive family members across the United States and Canada responded to a questionnaire or a phone or in-person interview for this book. This total included 12 birth grandparents, 93 adoptive parents, and 54 birth parents whose families represented children ranging in age from 6 months to a 26-year-old with children of her own. The families varied in age, in socio-economic status, and in city or country location, and included transracial and multicultural families, divorced and single parents, and gay and lesbian households. Although not all of their voices are directly heard in this book, many of the experiences they shared informed the writing. Many of the families that were chosen to be profiled reported doing well in managing these complex, challenging, and novel relationships. My intention was to let those who had the most experience in open adoption give us their perspective, their advice, and the benefit of their hindsight and wisdom. Their stories were chosen because they have much to tell us about what most helped their relationships work, and what values guided their decision making. Many of the family members have chosen to use first names only while others have shared their stories anonomously.

In addition to helping birth and adoptive parents consider open adoption from a child-centered perspective, the book attempts to educate adoption professionals about the needs of these complex families. Some of the families who responded to the questionnaires had access to experienced adoption professionals who offered excellent guidance and support, but many more felt that they were on their own in uncharted waters, and without much community support of their novel relationships. Those with younger children often voiced a need for more education and support about negotiating changes in contact, dealing with siblings, and handling conflicts. All of these issues should be part of an adoption education process that recognizes and supports the needs of these families both now and in the future.

My understanding of the "best practices" of open adoption has been developed by reading and listening to pioneering experts, especially Patricia Martinez Dorner, James Gritter, Lois Melina, Joyce Maguire Pavao, Brenda Romanchik, and Sharon Kaplan Roszia. These leaders in the field have had the courage, foresight, wisdom, and experience to challenge prevailing adoption practice by putting the child's needs back in the center of adoption. I hope that the material presented here will further enrich our understanding of how and why people make the choice to enter into these relationships, and once they do, how they evolve over time.

Families who have been living fully open adoption have much to teach us. Whether you are just beginning the adoption process, an expectant parent with an unplanned pregnancy, a birth or adoptive family already in an open relationship, an adoptive parent wanting to open a closed relationship, or an adoption professional, the families in this book want to speak with you. They want to speak about their challenges, their disappointments, the occasional logistical nightmares, and most of all, about their hopes and dreams for their children. For the sake of their child's ability to form an integrated sense of self, they have taken risks they never imagined they would take, opened themselves up to people they might not usually befriend, and formed ties that often last a lifetime. Theirs is a commitment that understood that giving children permanent, secure, and loving homes did not mean those children would have to lose their connection to the people who gave them life.

CHAPTER 1

My Family's Story

When I look at my daughter's beautiful face, her gorgeous curly hair, her expressive brown eyes, and her olive skin, I see her birth mother and whispers of another face, possibly her birth father's, someone whom I do not yet know. I say "not yet" because I have a link to her birth family and the full story is yet to be revealed.

When she was younger, people would come up to me in the store or on the street and ask me where she got her curls. I would usually say that I didn't know or that she inherited them. Her curls are likely to be noticed her entire life. When people ask her that question, I wonder if it will bring up the reality of adoption, as it is clear she did not get her curls from me. Many kids have curly hair and their biological parents do not. But for children who join families through adoption, questions such as these can encourage internal exploration. "Did my birth mother have curly hair? Where did I get the shape of my nose? Did someone else in my birth family love to dance? How old was my birth mother when she got her period? Are there any medical risks I should know about? What other parts of myself have been influenced by my birth family?"

When my husband and I began our adoption journey in the early 1990s, we lived in the Bay Area in California, one of the epicenters of openness in adoption. Like many prospective parents beginning the adoption process, we didn't know what to expect and needed help. As we educated ourselves about adoption we went to many workshops and symposiums, most of which were sponsored by the Northern California chapter of Resolve and local adoption agencies. It became clear to us that the identity issues for adopted children are profoundly impacted by the relationships they have or do not have with their birth families.

I distinctly remember one group of adults adopted as children speaking at a panel sponsored by Pact, an adoption organization specializing in education and support regarding transracial adoptions. One of the presenters who stood out was a young man in his early 20s who had recently met his birth father. He talked about the physical resemblance between him and his newly found birth father: the shape of the hands, the way their hair waved in similar ways. What caught him by surprise were the unexpected ways they resembled each other—the things that we don't usually attribute to genes. He said that it sent chills down his spine to hear a voice like his, from someone who tilted his head the same way he did. I was struck by this young man's response to the first meeting with his birth father. He wasn't certain if he needed or desired to have an ongoing relationship, but he knew that it was profoundly important that he had filled out this picture of himself. He said he felt whole in a way he had not imagined, because before meeting his birth father, he wasn't even aware that anything was missing. Feeling connected to who he was in a deeper way, he felt he could proceed with life with a richer sense of himself—a sense of himself that was no longer disconnected from the past.

In order to know who you are, you need to know something about where you came from; in order to move into the future, you have to be able to claim your past.

What moved me most about this bright and articulate young man was that even though he was totally at home with his adoptive family, he still found that having a link to his birth family met some deep and profound need. He loved his parents and felt strongly connected with his other siblings. School life had gone well for him, and he was in college, where he had many friends. It was precisely because of his apparent psychological health that I took his message to heart. In order to know who you are, you need to know something about where you came from; in order to move into the future, you have to be able to claim your past.

Looking back, I realize how important his message was to us. From the beginning, we viewed an adopted child as a baby who would fulfill our needs to parent, but also as a person who would grow into a teenager and an adult with particular needs related to adoption. We understood that a child of ours would have some of the same questions: "Where did I come from? Who created me?" I felt particularly drawn to other panels where birth parents and adult adoptees talked about the impact of adoption on their lives. What was clear from all of their stories was that adoption had a profound impact on their sense of identity and their experience of loss. My husband and I came to believe that having a direct link to one's biological, cultural, and ethnic heritage is a vital part of a person's identity. We wanted to give that to our child.

We were heavily influenced by the underlying message of many of the proponents of open adoption: that children would have a better psychological adjustment in life if they had relationships with their birth families. Many of the early proponents of openness had witnessed the effects of closed adoption on all members of the adoption triad. They had seen first hand the damaging impact of the closed system on birth parents and on the adopted children. A crucial leap in the history of adoption practice occurred when pioneering practitioners such as Rueben Pannor and Annette Baran, coauthors of The Adoption Triangle, began to break away from the secrecy and shame that shrouded closed adoptions. By the 1980's, the benefits of openness were often promoted, but without sound research to back up those claims. Nevertheless, the assumptions about the possible benefits made intrinsic sense to us.

In 1991, when we started the adoption process, we received no education from our adoption providers of how the relationships between birth and adoptive parents would evolve. While we embraced some of the ideas about the benefits of openness, we were relatively ignorant about how these relationships would develop over time. Neither my husband nor I carefully considered what an open adoption might look like in the future, either to ourselves, to the birth parents, or to the child. Although we wanted an open adoption, we wanted a baby even more. Questioning what kind of relationship we would or could develop in the future was far from our minds, as it is for many preadoptive parents.

It was in that context that we started our adoption journey. Adoption is often about stories: stories of how birth and adoptive families find one another, stories of loss and stories of reunion. Stories often make sense of what is not sensible; they give meaning to life events that are sometimes chaotic, and they plant us firmly in the realm of other humans that share our stories. It is in that context that I wish to share part of our adoption story, just as so many have shared their adoption stories with me in order to make this book possible.

I was 40 years old before I found a partner who shared my vision of becoming a family. Although I shouldn't have been, a few years later I was surprised to find myself in early menopause. As a teenager, I was very close to a family that had three adopted children so it didn't take much of a shift for me to turn in that direction. I thought that I did not have the time for a prolonged grieving process about the loss of a biological child. I just wanted to be a parent and move in the quickest way possible to get us there. After two years of sending out over 1,800 "Dear Birth Mother" adoption resumes, advertising throughout the country, and occasionally saying little prayers when dropping letters in the mailbox, we finally connected with a woman who was nine months pregnant.

Shortly after receiving our letter, "Elena" (not her real name) called and wanted to meet us as soon as possible. We made an airline reservation for the next night and waited at the airport with her name on a sign, but she never appeared. I had to go to a client's memorial (I was a therapist for people with AIDS at the time), so we drove home and my husband and 10-year-old stepdaughter returned to the airport, again waiting with the sign. The second plane arrived—no Elena. My husband came home again, dropped my stepdaughter off, and returned to the airport for the third time.

The last plane of the night arrived and Elena was on it! When I walked in the door of our home, my stepdaughter responded with a big smile and a thumbs up. I went into the living room and met a beautiful, charming, and good-humored woman. She was no longer in a relationship with the birth father, and did not want to be a single parent. Within minutes in her presence, I knew that I would be honored and blessed to give a life of love to her child.

The next day we made a medical appointment, since she had not had any prenatal care. The doctor pulled me aside after the exam and said that she was two centimeters dilated: "She could give birth in two weeks or two days." Later that night as we slept, I was awakened by Elena coming up the stairs to our bedroom. I jumped up and startled my husband awake as she came through the door on her knees saying, "I have much pain." My husband got a watch and we soon discovered that she was having contractions three to five minutes apart.

After two and a half years of waiting, after a roller-coaster of hope and despair, we had finally met this wonderful woman who was ready to give birth. A few hours later, with a scramble by the hospital team due to the speed of the delivery, a child began to enter the world. As the baby was being born, its back was toward me so I couldn't see whether it was a girl or a boy. I had wanted a daughter all my life, but in anxious anticipation of its being a boy, I found myself saying aloud, "It's a boy!" One of the nurses responded, "I don't know, it looks like a girl to me." It felt like a prayer had been answered.

We got to know Elena more as she spent the first week after the birth living with us. We talked about continuing contact through letters, phone calls, and visits, but we never talked about the benefits of staying in touch for the sake of the child. She seemed so open to continuing contact, that neither my husband nor I thought of underlining the future needs of the child to know her birth mother. After Elena left, we talked several times a week, which lessened to once a month as we became immersed in parenting an infant. We flew Elena to our home for our next visit when our daughter was eight months old. It was a wonderful visit where we had the chance to see Elena in a new context, and explain more fully our hopes and dreams for an ongoing relationship with her.

We explained that openness was a two-way street, and that she would also be deciding about how often we had contact, and how our relationship would evolve. My husband and I expressed empathy about the difficulty she might have as she separated from the baby, but also tried to stay in touch with us. We knew that she would face challenging emotions as she tried to remain open to the family of the child she had given birth to, but was not ready to parent.

We knew that she would face challenging emotions as she tried to remain open to the family of the child she had given birth to, but was not ready to parent.

Making Room in Our Hearts

As we were saying good-bye at the airport, I handed my daughter to her in a good-bye gesture and Elena broke down in tears. My heart went out to her as I could feel her anguish and the painful pull of separation, while at the same time she was trying to keep her heart open. Soon I was crying too, arms around my daughter and her birth mother, feeling the bittersweet joy and sadness inherent in adoption. As soon as she was home, I called her and told her that I understood that this was painful and she finished the sentence for me, "… but the other way is more painful."

Over the next two years, we made several attempts to fly Elena to visit us at our home, but she was unable to get on the plane, always with a last minute excuse of lost documents or a lost purse. After three failed attempts, we began making arrangements to fly to see her. She had since married and had not told her husband about the pregnancy or adoption. Being a Latina made it difficult for her to tell anyone in her family, especially her husband. Placing a child for adoption outside of one's extended family is generally viewed negatively within the Mexican-American community. We understood some of her concerns, and said we would meet her anywhere that would feel confidential to her. While in the last stage of making arrangements, we were greeted with a disconnected phone and no forwarding number. We made many attempts to reach her over the next year, all to no avail.

I soon began to feel the full weight of the loss to us and to my daughter's future. I had taken the messages about open adoption to heart and had deeply valued contact with my daughter's birth mother. I knew we could give my daughter all the love she would need to thrive. I could teach her about nature and the beauty of the earth; I could give her encouragement for self-expression; I could give her a community of wonderful people who would love her and value her special gifts. What I could not give her was her heritage, her connection to generations of people before her. I could not give her the experience of looking into the mirror and seeing that her face resembled others from her family. I had a dream about my daughter's possible future that was based on her having access to her birth family, and I was grieving the loss of that dream.

When I spoke to others about my feelings about losing contact with Elena, most people had similar responses: "She needed to move on. How could anyone give up a child and stay in touch? That would be torture!" or "You have a wonderful child, why can't you just be content with that?" The predominant message was that I should let go of my ideas about openness. People felt that the birth mother's behavior made it clear that either she did not really want an open relationship, or that she was not capable of maintaining the connection. No one seemed to understand the meaning and importance of trying to maintain a link to my daughter's past. Even the word *past* is too limited a concept when speaking about one's birth parents. The gifts one inherits from birth parents do not merely form the template, with the adoptive parents forming everything else. The personalities of adoptees are shaped throughout their lives by their biological and cultural roots.

Only by turning to several of the national experts in open adoption did I feel supported in my desire to connect and maintain contact with my daughter's birth mother. I had the opportunity to speak with Lois Melina, coauthor of *The Open Adoption Experience,* who was generous in her words of wisdom: "You are trying to lay the foundation for this open relationship by putting down one brick at a time. You hoped that your daughter's birth mother would have joined you in this effort, but she was unable to at this time. But that doesn't mean that you should stop laying the foundation." That analogy has come to my aid for several years. Trying to build this foundation is a gift for my daughter. I may not be able to finish it without some work on the part of her birth parents, but I can give her the gift of having tried to lay that foundation.

With this newfound validation, I continued to search. Elena had told us that a cousin of hers named Carlos (not his real name) had helped her with the adoption plan. When I reached him, he was friendly and generous, sharing stories about my daughter's birth mother. From what he said, it was clear that Elena was not capable of having a relationship at this time, but he understood that we wanted to keep the lines of communication open. He thought that Elena would be in touch with him eventually, and he was glad to receive our photos at his home where she could see them when she was ready. We were thankful for this vital connection and sent him appreciative cards with the photos.

Over the next 18 months, our phone calls became more frequent and more personal. One night he said: "You know, I am not really her cousin. Well, I am sort of a cousin because we have an aunt in common, but I was not just her relative." I didn't understand what he was trying to say so he tried to explain it again, but I was still missing the point. Finally, he said, "We were boyfriend and girlfriend for four years." I think he could tell from my startled silence that I was wondering what else he was. My head was spinning when he quickly added that he wasn't my daughter's birth father, but had supported Elena and helped her make the decision about adoption when she was pregnant. I was relieved that we now had a piece of the web from which my daughter's life began. As our relationship with Carlos developed, we were coming to terms with the fact that our hopes for open adoption were not possible, at least for now. My daughter had already passed the first seven years of her life without ongoing contact with her

The gifts one inherits from birth parents do not merely form the template, with the adoptive parents forming everything else. The personalities of adoptees are shaped throughout their lives by their biological and cultural roots.

Making Room in Our Hearts

birth mother. I wrote a keepsake letter to my daughter that included some of these feelings:

> Adoption is strange in some ways. I look at you and cannot imagine that you didn't come out of my body because you are so much a part of me now. But I do know that you did not come from me. I see your birth mother in your face—sometimes I can see her eyes, her lips, her smile, and even feel her laughter. I feel loving feelings toward her in many ways. She is my daughter's mother—my daughter is her daughter. Her flesh is now of my flesh. Her creation is my joy. We are bound together through the most powerful love of a mother for her child. She will always be part of me as you are part of her. How could I not love her?

The relationship with Carlos has continued to evolve and at his suggestion, we spent a wonderful day with him, his girlfriend, and his niece and nephew at Disneyland. After a few moments of shyness, my daughter and he were inseparable, connecting as though they had known each other for years. Since that visit, he has been as attentive as any family member could be: sending her cards and gifts and calling every few months. A year later, during another visit, my hands were sweating as I broached the sensitive subject of whether Carlos might be my daughter's birth father. He again denied that he was, and seemed concerned that if he were the birth father, he would have to be more involved in parenting. I explained that the relationship we had established was wonderful just as it was. He had become a loving link to her heritage and she was obviously a very special child to him. What more could we ask?

Carlos consistently alludes to the special relationship he has with my daughter. On a recent phone call he said, "Even though I am not her daddy, she feels like a daughter to me. I will always be in her life." Once at the end of a visit, he jokingly offered some hair for DNA analysis. After hesitating briefly, I didn't accept it. I thought DNA testing should be done only after careful consideration of the implications for him, for my husband and me, and for my daughter. For now, I have accepted that Carlos is our only connection to my daughter's birth family and I am thankful for it. We have laid the bricks for this foundation and have created a partial retaining wall, knowing that we have a connection that could help us in the future.

I do not know where these steps will lead. Will we ever make contact with Elena? Will we eventually request a DNA test to determine if Carlos is her birth father? To what extent will we advocate for contact with other members of my daughter's large extended birth family when her birth mother is not able or willing to build a relationship? How far should we go to help my daughter deal with the missing links in her life? I don't know where these questions will lead, but I am certain that however this turns out, the knowledge that we gain will continue to assist our daughter as she constructs her ever-evolving sense of self.

The loss of contact with my daughter's birth mother creates grief that we are not only anticipating for the future, but are experiencing in the present. Shortly after her eighth birthday, my daughter was dancing in the living room, joyously moving to the rhythms of her new *Lion King* CD. The next time I looked, she was sitting on the couch, clutching the picture of her birth mother, which she had taken from her bedroom. I approached her and found her crying uncontrollably. I asked what had brought all this on, and she said there was a song about the circle being broken that reminded her of her birth mother leaving her and never returning. Her tears did not seem like those of a child—they seemed as profound as any grief I have ever witnessed in an adult. Barely able to speak through the sobs, she said, "I can't bear this pain." These were not words she was accustomed to hearing. There was not much we could do but hold her in our arms and tell her we understood that it must be very painful to not know the person who gave birth to you. These moments pass and she goes on to live her happy, spirited, and expressive life, surrounded by love from many people. I understand that her feelings of loss are one of the painful parts of adoption, but it is also a loss that we had hoped might be somewhat lessened by contact with her birth family.

Many people are navigating the waters of openness not because they think it will make the pain of adoption disappear, but because they believe it will enhance the child's sense of self. They have come to believe that it is part of children's birth right to know more about those who created them: their history, their decision-making about adoption, their concern for the child, and their dreams for the future. They are often doing this without lessons on how to row the boat, and with little means of communicating with others who are entering the same waters. The families profiled here didn't know what the outcome would be for them or their children. They all took a certain degree of risk because they understood the importance of families of origin in shaping the identities of their children.

Families in fully open adoption are challenging social norms and broadening this society's definitions of what it means to make and become family. They are saying that they will not be put into neatly circumscribed categories with clearly drawn lines between the birth family and the adoptive family. They are creating extended familial relationships that are unique to their own histories, needs, and desires. By listening to their experiences, by hearing the variety of the ways that these families have coped, we can see what open adoption is like over time. These families are letting us into their lives so we can see the diversity, the richness, and the challenges that are part of open adoption.

> *Many people are navigating the waters of openness not because they think it will make the pain of adoption disappear, but because they believe it will enhance the child's sense of self.*

Making Room in Our Hearts

CHAPTER 2

Into the Heart of Child-Centered Open Adoption

When we look into the heart of adoption we see a child, but when a woman and man are facing an unplanned pregnancy, or a couple has struggled with infertility and turns to adoption, they both see that baby through the lens of *their own needs*. The adoptive parents have usually been waiting for years to have a baby to love and cherish. They are most likely not thinking about the day when the child may wonder what personality characteristics she inherited from her birth parents. The woman with a crisis pregnancy is also caught up in the needs of the moment and is usually confused, overwhelmed, and scared. However, the nature of *her* dilemma forces her to look into the future in order to decide if she will be able to parent. This chapter will look at how birth and adoptive parents bridge the differences between them, examine lessons from the closed system, reflect on identity formation and loss, and discuss a child-centered view of openness. This will be followed by a profile of a birth and adoptive family whose members have been in relationship with each other for 15 years.

Coming Together

Placing a child for adoption is a parenting decision made by women and men who are often in crisis and without adequate emotional or financial support. Most birth parents do not want to "give up" their children. What they want is to alleviate the situation that they find themselves in; namely, an inability, for whatever reason, to adequately parent and provide for a child at a particular time. After assessing their situation, they have come to the often wrenchingly painful conclusion that it would be better for this child to be raised by someone who is ready to parent. It may come as a surprise to them that they can have some say in choosing who will parent their child, and most often they do not expect to form ongoing relationships with the adoptive family. Their adoption providers may have talked with them about staying in contact, but may not have discussed the ongoing role they might play in their child's life.

Adoptive parents have frequently spent years on what is an exhausting treadmill of infertility treatments, and as a result, their emotional, spiritual, and financial resources have usually taken a beating. Their baby hunger is so strong that they would climb mountains to be able to parent, and open adoption may feel just like that: a formidable mountain to climb. When one has been waiting so long to have a child, the inclination is to circle the wagons, get a baby, and close the circle in order to claim that child as one's own. Openness may be viewed as lessening the right of the adoptive parents to become what they have waited so long to become: authentic parents. After having experienced infertility as an personal intrusion, the idea of opening their lives to a birth family is often overwhelming. They also may be fearful of having a child reclaimed, and in their minds, openness may increase the risks of this taking place.

When they start from such different and vulnerable places, what brings birth parents and adoptive parents together? A myriad of factors have contributed to the movement toward openness in adoption, one of which is necessity. Adam Pertman in *Adoption Nation* (2000) discusses the broad sociological and political forces that contributed to a vast change in the landscape of adoption. In the mid-twentieth century, the vast majority of women with unwanted pregnancies placed their children for adoption. In 2000, less than 3% of women in the same circumstances turned to adoption as a solution to an undesired pregnancy. Among the many factors contributing to the decrease in adoption, was the increasing availability of legalized abortion and society's increased acceptance of single parenthood. Adoption agencies were faced with the stark reality that there were far more people looking for children to adopt than there were women placing their children for adoption.

This vast sociological shift occurred during the same period that we were hearing the voices of those most impacted by the practices of the closed system. In the '60s and '70s, birth parents and adopted persons were beginning to raise their collective voices about the psychological and spiritual damage done to them by the worst practices of closed adoption.

Joining the voices of protest were adoption professionals who had worked in the closed system and experienced first hand the negative impact of that system on all members of the adoption triad. Some professionals, especially Annette Baran and Rueben Pannor, were instrumental in the movement toward more openness in adoption. They began to advocate for a more humane approach that allowed additional information to be passed

In the '60s and '70s, birth parents and adopted persons were beginning to raise their collective voices about the psychological and spiritual damage done to them by the worst practices of closed adoption.

Making Room in Our Hearts

between birth and adoptive parents, gradually leading to contact between the parties. Birth parents, especially birth mothers, were beginning to express their desire to participate in the decision-making process about who would become the parents of their child. Gradually, some courageous professionals and agencies began to change their practices in the direction of more openness. When given the choice, birth parents frequently chose the path of more openness, and agencies around the country were forced to change or lose referrals.

Lessons from the Closed System

Under the closed system, the issues surrounding adoption were encased in the bureaucratic concrete of misguided social policies. These policies added to the already heavy burden of unwanted pregnancies and infertility. The fact of "illegitimacy" was viewed as shameful by the larger culture, and supported by adoption practices that further undermined the power of the most crucial players in this intensely human drama: the birth parents. Birth mothers were frequently sent away from their base of social support to complete the pregnancy, denied truthful information about the adoptive family, and allowed no participation in the decision-making process. Many pregnant women were told at birth that it would be best if they did not see their baby, and shields were sometimes erected to keep them from witnessing the birth of their own child. Occasionally, even the knowledge of the baby's gender was withheld in an attempt to "protect" the birth mother from the emotional pain that might prevent her from following through with her decision.

Adoption agencies made all the decisions about which family would receive the baby, and neither party received more than the sketchiest information about the other. Birth parents were told to close the emotional doors in order to move on, to forget about their relinquished child so they could start life anew. Placing a child for adoption is one of the most profound events of a woman's life and has psychological reverberations far beyond the relinquishment of the child. Yet, rarely did birth parents receive counseling from their adoption agencies as they struggled with the grief, shame, or remorse they may have felt about their decision. What seemed like sound social work advice at the time, was in fact, a recipe for a future mental health disaster. Many birth mothers from the closed system report that although they moved on, they were never able to fully come to terms with the loss and its effect on their lives.

Gail, a 44-year-old birth mother remembers:

> There has not been a day in my life since the birth of my son 27 years ago that I have not thought of him. How is he doing? What does he look like? Does he feel loved? I really don't know if he is dead or alive. To have such a part of you taken away with no information has

always felt like an amputation. Yes, I wasn't ready to be a mother, but I also wasn't ready to have my heart torn out of me. Adoption in the old days was like being banished to a kind of hell. I feel like I was being forever punished for the simple fact that I had sex too young and got pregnant.

Mary Anne was a vivacious and charismatic woman who struggled with a life-threatening illness with humor and gusto. As she approached the end stage of her disease, she grew more pensive about the daughter she had placed for adoption over 11 years before. Before her illness, she had made several attempts at locating the adoptive family, but was told by the adoption agency that all the records had been lost. Always wanting more control over life than she had, she wrote the words that were to be read at her own funeral, and the first ones were addressed to the child she had placed for adoption: "My dear Tamara: I do not know you, but you are part of me. Please know that wherever you are, I have carried you in my heart for all these years and always wondered how you were doing. I am sorry I did not get to meet you before I had to leave."

Under the closed system, adoptive parents were also less than adequately prepared for the realities of adoption. They were often told to behave like a "normal family," but adoptive families *are* different and have unique needs and challenges. Children were seen as starting their life as a "blank slate" that would be written upon solely by the nurturing and love of the adoptive parents. This left adoptive parents in the dark when their children began to experience the losses inherent in adoption. Adoptive parents were often instructed to tell children about adoption in ways that undermined the reality of their origins. Being told a story throughout your childhood that you were "chosen" would later be understood to mean you were "*un*chosen" by the people who gave you life. (Melina, 1998) Just as the closed system kept birth and adoptive parents from knowing each other's identity, it also kept vital medical information from being passed to the adoptive family.

In the *The Open Adoption Experience*, by Lois Melina and Sharon Kaplan Roszia, the authors underscore the effects of the closed system:

> It gradually became apparent through research, personal accounts, and case histories, that the failure to recognize and grieve for the losses of adoption had long term effects. Some adoptees had impaired self-esteem because they were unable to shake the belief that they were rejected by their [birth] mothers. Some had difficulty forming an identity because they did not know who they were. Some had difficulty forming relationships because they did not understand why they had lost a primary relationship with their birth parents. Not all confidential adoptions were failures, nor did all adoptees, birth

To have such a part of you taken away with no information has always felt like an amputation. Yes, I wasn't ready to be a mother, but I also wasn't ready to have my heart torn out of me.

— Gail,
a 44-year-old
birth mother

Making Room in Our Hearts

parents and adoptive parents suffer serious psychological problems. However, there were many people who found that their experience of adoption provided them with emotional challenges that they did not expect and didn't always know how to conquer. (page 6)

The old version of adoption had happy adoptive parents smiling into the camera with their new baby. Not only were the birth parents not in the picture, they literally and figuratively, were not anywhere to be seen in the whole photo album. It was as though they had disappeared, and in many cases, that is exactly what happened. The closed system was a disservice to all members of the adoption triad. It kept birth parents from being able to acknowledge the depth of their loss and offered few resources to help them come to terms with their decision. Birth mothers who longed to know more about how their child was doing were left with gaping wounds. It left adoptive families without full entitlement to be parents, as they were given few tools to assist their children in developing their whole identity. And the children were left wondering: Who am I? Who made me? What are my birth parents like? Where did I get my nose? Was my father musical too? And why did they make the decision that they couldn't raise me?

Identity Formation

When we look closely into the heart of adoption, we can see a child who will have questions about her origins and who will someday understand that the family tree that represents her life is different from that of others. The roots of the adopted person's family tree represent the biological and ethnic heritage they received from their birth parents. The branches of the tree represent their adoptive family and all the nurturing that will allow them to flourish and grow. We know that at the heart of open adoption is not just a child, but one who was created and given life by one family and parented by another. That child will grow up and become a teenager and an adult, with all the challenges of incorporating these two different realities into his or her identity.

Identity is a complex issue for all of us. Discovering who we are, learning to accept our strengths and limitations, and feeling good about ourselves is a lifelong process. All of us, adopted or not, face losses that influence us forever: curves in the road, not of our own making, that often determine the course of our future. But for children who join families through adoption, Lois Melina emphasizes that the quest for wholeness is more complicated:

Every person who has been adopted must come to terms with the fact that the people who were supposed to take care of him made a decision that they could not. Every adoptee evaluates whether this affects his

There were many people who found that their experience of adoption provided them with emotional challenges that they did not expect and didn't always know how to conquer.

— Lois Melina and Sharon Kaplan Roszia

worth as a human being or his ability to attract people who will love and commit to him. (1998)

Kinship Center is an adoption agency that includes educational and counseling services supportive of open adoption. At the Kinship Center's training on clinical issues in adoption, a video is presented that incudes Joey Nesler who was adopted in the closed system and is now a therapist working in adoption. This is what she has to say about the experience of living without knowledge of her origins:

> Not knowing anyone from my birth family felt like I was a puddle: isolated and disconnected. Reunification is like finally becoming part of a river. I have a sense that I am part of something dynamic that came before and will go on after. This is every person's birthright. It is not just the right of nonadopted persons. I am a human being. I have the same needs as all other human beings. I have the right to know where I am in the stream of life. (Joey Nesler, personal communication, 2004)

We know from research and from what adopted people have said about their lives, that severing the ties to their birth family often creates a vulnerability to loss. For some adoptees, these vulnerabilities are like jagged-peaked mountains that must be climbed, with thickly forested valleys that must be crossed, and they often suffer angst and confusion along the way. For others, these vulnerabilities are more lightly imprinted and the feelings of loss connected to adoption are handled with relative ease. But for all adopted persons, forming a whole identity, weaving a story about their lives from their adoptive family with the strands from their family of origin, is often a psychologically challenging task.

Saying that adoption complicates the search for self does not mean that adoption is necessarily detrimental to the development of a strong and cohesive sense of self. Many of us have faced profound losses in childhood that challenge us to grow and point us in certain directions. Even when losses take us to our knees, it is how we stand up again that builds our capacity for resilience in the face of challenge. Loss is not only a deficit in life: it can mold and strengthen us like clay in the hands of a fine potter, breathing resilience into our being. And like all other major challenges in life, adoption entails both losses and blessings, confusions and certainties, instability and security.

Each child who has joined a family through adoption has inherited unique characteristics and has been impacted by a variety of factors. Prenatal influences such as nutrition, drug exposure, stress, and the emotional state of the birth mother during the pregnancy all impact the child's ability to adapt to life with a new set of parents. For the adoptive family, readiness to parent, resolution of the couple's infertility issues, and attitudes about adoption all

Every person who has been adopted must come to terms with the fact that the people who were supposed to take care of him made a decision that they could not.

— Lois Melina

Making Room in Our Hearts

impact their ability to welcome a child into their home and claim it as their own. Therefore, every adopted child faces the task of growing up with a unique set of strengths and vulnerabilities, some inherited, others influenced by prenatal exposure, and some from their adoptive family. Every adopted child will have his or her own unique concerns and questions about the relationship of his adoption to his developing sense of self.

At the same time that adoptive parents honor the individuality and uniqueness of their children, they need to acknowledge the additional complexity that adopted children face in the formation of their identity. David Brodzinsky, Ph.D., is an expert on the psychological development of adopted people, and has spent his career studying the issues that confront adopted children and adults. When asked what percentage of adoptees search for their birth parents, he replies, "One hundred percent." Brodzinsky points out that the search for one's birth parents involves much more than the actual process of attempting to locate them in a geographical sense. Rather, the search is part of a psychological journey, and it is one that adopted people are involved in at different stages of their lives, and may or may not include an actual search.

The awareness of birth parents being "out there somewhere," continually shifts from the background to the foreground for an adopted child. When my daughter was 5, she and I were on the Bay Area's subway and she leaned over and whispered to me about a woman across the aisle, "Doesn't she look like my birth mother?" I doubt that she was searching crowds looking for any face that might be her birth mother's, but she was vigilant enough to notice when she saw a woman who had a clear resemblance to a picture of her birth mother. The awareness that someone intimately related to you is out there, but you do not know where, is often part of the consciousness of an adopted person. For those who know nothing about their origins, the tendency to try to fill in the picture with fantasizing can be very strong.

Ben, at age 29, presented his feelings about adoption and identity in a particularly moving story. He had been placed for adoption when he was 9 months old, during the years of the closed system. When he was 7, he was shown a picture of himself as a baby that had been given to the adoptive parents through the adoption agency. The picture had clearly been cropped to remove other people. Who were they? His birth mother? His birth grandparents?

> For years, I stared at that picture. I turned it over, upside down, and sideways. I wanted to turn it inside out so I could see what was hidden from me. I peered at it from all possible directions. I turned it over just so slightly, hoping against hope that it would reveal the missing people in the picture. I scanned the photo looking for clues

This is every person's birthright. It is not just the right of nonadopted persons. I have the right to know where I am in the stream of life.

— Joey Nesler

that might help me understand who they were, who I was, who I am. I would examine the furniture in the photo to figure out what kind of people they were. I did the same thing with my birth certificate, even up until my early twenties. For some reason it was white print on black paper. I was convinced that there was some secret code or hidden impression on the paper that would include my birth mother's name. I held it up to the light, scanning for anything that would help me uncover my true identity.

Because many adopted persons wonder, search, and fantasize about birth families does not mean that they do not love and value their parents. Ben continued,

> It's not that I didn't feel loved. I love my parents and my family and my two siblings. But my whole life, I have felt like I was different, not quite in the club of normal people. Adoption has been sort of like a shadow over my life. I have always wondered, how could she do it? What was so wrong that after almost 10 months with me, she gave me away? Who would I have been if I had grown up in that other family? If I knew who my birth mother was, I could have stopped the fantasizing and wondering. She would have been real and I could have just asked her those questions instead of having them bounce around in my head for all those years.

What Is Child-Centered Open Adoption?

Child centered open adoption is just that: all those who are concerned with an adoption, whether they are the birth parents, adoptive parents, or adoption agency personnel, consider that the child's current and future needs are at the very center of the adoption process. It is for the child that an adoption decision was made, and it is for the child's identity that relationships are developed and maintained. Child-centered adoption means keeping family ties when they are appropriate, and creating healthy boundaries between birth and adoptive families in order to maintain those ties. Child-centered adoption means remembering that the child is of two worlds, and for that child to grow up as one integrated person, he or she will have the task of putting these worlds together. Adoptive parents and birth parents can help adopted children weave these worlds into a cohesive braid that is the reality of their lives as adopted persons.

Parents who understand the psychological tasks for their adopted child, can honor the birth family as an important part of their child's identity. To deny the birth family's importance, is to deny the child his or her right to wholeness. Although birth parents were not ready to parent, they have a vital role to play in helping their child know that she was loved *then* and is loved *now* by those who gave her life.

Fully open adoption often includes contact between family members outside the adoption triad: a birth grandmother who makes an annual present for the child's birthday; an aunt who holds the connection when the birth mother is unable to do so; the adoptive grandparent who makes a unique connection with the birth grandmother. For some, this will sound just like most families: contacts, roles, and relationships shifting over time. For others, it may raise concerns: how will I be able to open my life to an entire group of people who are strangers to me now?

Prospective adoptive parents are not alone if they have concerns, questions, or fears about open adoption. Most of the families interviewed did not start out assuming that they would become extended family with each other. Some were pleased by the ease with which their families came to know each other, and they remain surprised by the ease through the passing years. For many, the need to pull back and lessen contact at times has been an important part of keeping the relationships alive. Each extended family has created its own unique blend of openness that works for that specific group of people.

Openness Takes Away Mystery and Shame

The following profile gives us a glimpse into the healing potential of open relationships, even for those who suffered shame under the closed system. What started out as a closed adoption shrouded in secrecy, is now a vibrant extended family. Debbi is the birth mother of Danny, age 20, and Diane is the adoptive mother. They have been in contact since Danny was 6 years old.

Debbi, Birth Mother to Danny

Open adoption was not even a remote possibility when I was pregnant in Kansas in the early '80s. Not being able to know that my son was healthy and happy was excruciating, and a day never went by that I didn't think about him. I wasn't sitting around crying though, because I had stuffed the pain down too far. When I thought of him, the visual part was blank because I never saw him after he was born. The nurses recommended that I not see or hold him because it would make it too painful to give him up. That actually made it harder to grieve because I couldn't even picture him in my mind.

I have beaten myself up for years for not having had the courage to ask to see my baby, but I have to remind myself that the professionals who were helping me, did not encourage this. I didn't even have a name to remember because no one asked me if I wanted to name him. I wish someone could have spoken with me about grief, but instead, I felt like

Although birth parents were not ready to parent, they have a vital role to play in helping their child know that she was loved then and is loved now by those who gave her life.

From left to right: Debbi, Danny and Diane. Diane is Danny's adoptive mother and Debbi is his birth mother.

> *The nurses recommended that I not see or hold him because it would make it too painful to give him up. That actually made it harder to grieve because I couldn't even picture him in my mind.*
>
> — Debbi, a birth mother

I was left with nothing but a dirty little secret. It wasn't until years later that I realized this pain was felt by my parents and friends as they also felt unequipped to handle the pain and loss.

Five years later, I was married and starting a family when feelings about my birth son were reawakened. I had done a lot of emotional work trying to fill the hole left from the adoption, but raising my first daughter made me revisit my feelings about the child I had given up. I wrote a letter to the adoption attorney explaining that I needed to know how my son was doing. Three days later I was speechless when I received a letter and pictures from my son's mother, Diane, and over the next several weeks we had more contact. During this time, my husband was transferred to Hutchinson, Kansas and I didn't know it at the time, but my birth son, Danny, lived in the same town.

After we moved, his mother suggested that we meet. I was so nervous, but she was so comfortable in her role as his mother that I knew we could work it out. After lunch, she asked if I wanted to join her to pick

Making Room in Our Hearts

Danny up from school. What could I say? I was worried that I might cry and I didn't want to scare him. When he got in the car, I could hardly turn my head to look at him, but I was overjoyed! I realized at that moment that this adoption was not about my pain or about Diane and her husband's gain of a child. It was about my son Danny.

Some healing happened that day for me. It took place the moment I looked at him and saw in his eyes that he was happy and had a passion for life. What more could I want?

When we finally told Danny who I was, he took it very casually, saying, "So that is why I look like you." I think he had felt there was something special between us and we definitely looked alike. His parents and I talked about our concerns before we moved forward. We were worried that in his teen years Danny might play us against each other, but that has never happened. He has always been very clear about who his parents are.

Some members of Danny's extended adoptive family were afraid that I might be invasive or threaten the adoptive relationships that had been established. But when they met me, they realized I wasn't a threat because I had my own family, and I only wanted what was the best for Danny. My parents were also afraid that the doors might close and I would be wounded all over again. With time, they all grew to understand that this relationship was based on our mutual love for Danny. Gradually, we became an extended family, and my husband Rick has been extraordinary in his love for Danny and his ability to include him in our family.

When Danny was 8 years old, his parents divorced. That was really hard for me. For a while, I questioned the adoption decision since so much of it had to do with my not wanting to be a single parent. But I knew that he still had a life filled with love and that I couldn't control the situation. By the time he was 12, we started having more of an independent relationship, and Danny started spending a few nights a year with our family, and he also began to get closer to my daughters. I told my daughters that Danny was their half-brother and they seem to have taken this in their stride. If asked, I would say he is their half-brother, but *they* would never say that. When my oldest daughter did a picture of her family for class, she included Danny as her brother.

Sure, there have been some challenges, but who doesn't have any of those? When Danny was 17, he asked if he could meet his birth father. That was painful for me because it brought up all the stuff from the past. The relationship with Danny's parents had been so healing for me, and I didn't want to go backwards into the shame of the past. Dealing with people's judgment has also been difficult, but Diane and I have

I realized at that moment that this adoption was not about my pain or about Diane and her husband's gain of a child. It was about my son Danny.

— Debbi

become allies in our role as educators about open adoption, and have grown to relish the astonishment on people's faces.

What has made it work so well is understanding our different roles in Danny's life. Diane has always been confident in her role as his mother. Her purpose in opening this up was never to share parenting. As much as I believe in my decision to have relinquished my parental rights, it is still a little hard to say "I am not his mother—I am his birth mother." But I would not go back and change anything. I love Danny and the many parts of him that have been formed by his adoptive parents. He isn't the same person he would have been if I had raised him, and I love him for who he is now.

At the same time, Danny and I are both proud of the fact that we look so much alike. I listen to him and I can hear a familiar voice from my own family. We have always had a string between our hearts and no one, not even adoption, can break those ties. Those ties last forever.

I love Danny and the many parts of him that have been formed by his adoptive parents. He isn't the same person he would have been if I had raised him, and I love him for who he is now.

— Debbi

Danny at Age 21

I have known my birth mother as long as I can remember and I can't imagine it any other way. I would be a completely different person if I had grown up without knowing who I was and where I came from. Open adoption has allowed me to be the person I was intended to be—with a connection to the people who made me what I am. Most adoptive parents might not be as open as my mother has been, but it just hasn't been threatening to her because she is definitely my mother and she knows that. Besides, if you are a kid's parent, wouldn't you want to help him figure out who he is? I have never felt any conflicts about relating to both of them. I think of Debbi as my Mom, but she definitely isn't my parent.

Most people in Kansas have no idea about how this works, so when I tell people, it knocks them off their feet for a second. I had a girlfriend in high school who had a problem with it. My birth mother came to my graduation party, and that was the first time my girlfriend met her. She thought that it was wrong and that we should not acknowledge each other. I have known this almost my whole life and I don't have any sense of having to hide it—it is just part of who I am. Hey, this is just another alternative lifestyle.

We took personality tests my senior in high school and it piqued my curiosity to know what I had inherited from my birth father. I had considered meeting him, but I had talked myself out of it because I was afraid that it might bring up all this pain about the past for my birth mom. After discussing my doubts with Debbi, we decided that we would meet. That was one of the most exciting and anxious times of my

From left to right: Debbi and Danny. Debbi is Danny's birth mother.

life, and I was sweating bullets as we waited for him in the restaurant. When he finally arrived, he and Debbi had to talk because I was so nervous the only thing I could do was eat. I am glad that I met the man that was partially responsible for my birth, but that is how I see him— as a biological dad. You can only have a birth parent if they have a role to play in your life. I have a real relationship with my birth mother and that has made all the difference in the world.

You can only have a birth parent if they have a role to play in your life. I have a real relationship with my birth mother and that has made all the difference in the world.

— Danni,
age 21

Diane, Danny's Adoptive Mother

My advice to adoptive and birth parents is to know from the start that open adoption is not shared parenting. I have never had any doubt that I am Danny's mother. The fact that we had the first several years to bond before we connected with his birth mother made a big difference. But I think what made the biggest difference is the kind of person Debbi is—she is totally trustworthy. By the time she contacted us, she had made a life for herself and I simply had no fears about her invading ours. If she had been 15, addicted to drugs, or was invasive, I don't think it would have worked. Open adoption isn't for everyone—you have to be able to trust that person.

I was receptive to Debbie's request for contact because I always felt that an adopted child is not just your own child. Birth parents are a part of who your child is and sooner or later, the child will want to find out more. I just thought that Danny should be able to have as much love in his life as possible with people he could depend upon. He knows Debbi cares deeply about him and will listen endlessly to him. I am sure there are things that he tells her that he may not tell us, but I am glad he has that in his life. Open adoption has taken all the mystery away and helped Danny know himself better.

It hasn't always been as easy for other members of my family. It was hard for my first husband because he felt protective and a little jealous about the closeness that Danny and I were developing with Debbi. Later, when we were getting divorced, I was embarrassed to tell Debbi that our marriage wasn't going to survive. But those things happen in many families. We also had challenging times when Danny was 13 and we moved to Colorado with my second husband. It was a difficult time for Danny to be leaving his friends and his birth mother. Debbi saw the pain Danny was in and voiced her concerns to me. It was the first time that she gave her opinion about a parenting decision, but she didn't do it to interfere, she was just concerned about Danny. I felt guilty that the move had affected him so badly, but I knew we had to do it. Those are the kinds of decisions parents need to make and I have no doubt that I am his parent.

Open adoption can only work if both birth and adoptive parents want some of the same things. I advise adoptive parents to put the child's needs first and not let their fears control them, but I also know that people shouldn't go beyond their limits. If you are being nice to birth parents, but don't really feel it, it won't work out. These have to be genuine relationships, not something based on a theory. Look at us—we were doing this when there were no books, no experts, we had no idea of what we were "supposed" to do. It has worked because of trust and mutual respect. You have got to remember that your child has a life that will go on after yours has ended, and he or she won't be a baby forever. But helping children know who they are will last them a lifetime. (Debbi, Diane, and Danny: personal communication 2004 and 2005)

> *You have got to remember that your child has a life that will go on after yours has ended, and he or she won't be a baby forever. But helping children know who they are will last them a lifetime.*
>
> — Diane, an adoptive mother

CHAPTER 3

Understanding Each Other's Fears and Concerns

In my eight years as a facilitator for adoption support groups, I have worked with many couples and individuals as they begin the adoption process. When I talk about maintaining connections with birth families, I can see the shoulders of many in the room begin to tighten. The first reaction of many preadoptive parents is to see a relationship with a birth family as a threat to their own parenting. For expectant parents, dealing with grief and trying to keep connected, may seem like an impossible task. This chapter will look at some of the research to see how it addresses the misconceptions about open adoption. We will then look at some of the fears and concerns that birth and adoptive parents face as they consider open adoption: coping with grief, keeping agreements about contact, claiming the right to parent, and wondering if the child will be confused. Following this, the profiled family features a young man who is very clear about his own needs: "I didn't want to have a pen-pal birth mother. I wanted a real person."

Research

The research that tells us most about open adoption is that done by Grotevant and McRoy (1998) who looked at a total of 721 birth mothers, adoptive parents, and adopted children and 35 adoption agencies from 1987 to 2004. Their research findings which covered the years 1987 to 1992, are described in *Openness in Adoption: Exploring Family Connections*. This is the most in-depth longitudinal study to date of the full range of adoption from confidential or closed (no exchange of information); to mediated sharing (sharing of information through the adoption agency); to fully disclosed adoptions (direct sharing of information and meetings between adoptive family and birth parents). Following are some of the major findings of their research:

- The vast majority of adoptive parents who chose openness were very satisfied with their choices. If anything, they desired more contact with the birth parents, not less. Adoptive parents in fully disclosed adoption communicate more with their child about adoption, are able to empathize more with the birth parents and the child about their own losses, and are more accepting of the child's curiosity regarding adoption. Overall, adoptive parents in fully open adoptions felt a greater sense of permanence in their relationship to their child, and were less afraid of the child being reclaimed by the birth parents.
- Birth parents were found to be more satisfied with their role in relation to the adoptive parents and the adopted child in fully disclosed adoptions. They also felt a greater sense of personal control, and there was less post placement depression and a lessened grief reaction following placement. In the follow-up of this study, it was found that for most birth mothers, the more open the adoption, the greater the birth mother's satisfaction. The authors were careful to state, however, *that no one type of adoption was the right one for every birth parent's needs.*
- Children in fully open adoption show a better understanding of adoption, have expressed more curiosity about their birth parents, had more of their questions answered, and felt that they had more permission to explore the meaning of adoption in their lives. Most importantly, the adjustment of children was shown to be better for those who experienced collaborative relationships between the adoptive parents and the birth parents.

In the second wave of the research that covered the years 1995–2000, the authors concluded that: "Collaboration is characterized by the ability of the child's adoptive and birthparents to work together effectively on behalf of the child's well-being. It involves collaborative control over the way in which contact is handled and is based on mutual respect, empathy and valuing of the relationship" (2002). Working together for the sake of the child seems to work best for everyone, but how do we get there?

Our daughter's birth mother appreciates our lack of judgment about her life, which is none too stable. We just accept her for who she is and that makes it work.

— Ellen, an adoptive parent

In the Beginning: Making a Commitment

Birth and adoptive parents come together because they each want what the other one has: the birth parents want people who are ready and able to parent, and the individual or couple want a child. It may seem like these different positions would make for a competitive relationship, and in some cases it does. But when we look at these people staying together *for the sake of the child,* we arrive at a different kind of arrangement.

The authors of *The Open Adoption Experience* compare the relationship commitment between adoptive parents and birth parents with in-laws:

People meet their in-laws with the understanding that they will be entering into a long-term relationship primarily because they both love and are concerned for the well being of the same person. They may have different values. They may have different lifestyles. But often, even before getting to know each other very well, they make a commitment to making the relationship work because doing so is in the best interest of someone else, to whom their commitment is firmly established. (page 20)

To make that commitment, adoptive and birth parents first need to address their fears and concerns.

Dealing with Grief and Staying in Touch

A major concern for birth parents is that it will be too painful to stay involved with the relinquished child while not being able to parent. Friends and family often reinforce this view. One mother told her daughter, "How can you tear away from this baby, then expect to be able to see it without it eating you up?" As we have seen, closed adoption practices supported this view, and women were discouraged from holding the baby, assuming that if they didn't get close, it would be easier. However, we know that closed adoption did not offer birth parents an easier resolution to their grief. Peggy, a 43-year-old birth mother, had this to say: "There hasn't been one day in the 20 years of my birth son's life, that I haven't thought about him. If I could have seen and known him, it wouldn't have remained such a painful thorn in my mind." Even though closed adoptions are diminishing, there remains a strong cultural belief that the sooner the birth mother can put the birth and adoption behind her, the better. Many of the birth parents interviewed for this book realized that it would be painful to see their child with someone else, but felt that the pain of complete separation would have made it impossible to consider adoption.

Many of the birth parents interviewed for this book realized that it would be painful to see their child with someone else, but felt that the pain of complete separation would have made it impossible to consider adoption.

Grotevant and McRoy's research (1998) supports this view:

About 70% of birthmothers recalled having mixed or ambivalent feelings during their first meeting. They felt a combination of sadness as well as reassurance about the child's well-being. Clearly the meetings seemed to help many birthmothers resolve some of the pain, hurt, guilt, and sad feelings over the placement of their children. (p.145) Contrary to the predictions of critics, the opportunity to see the child with the adoptive family seemed to have a "healing effect." Many birth parents claimed that they were better able to accept their decision to make an adoption plan once they knew that the child was happy. (page 149)

When birth parents have no contact with the adoptive family, they have little opportunity to form a sense of themselves as valuable people with a unique role to play in the adoptive family's life. Adoptive parents can turn to well-established networks of support, but there is little in the way of community support for birth parents. Many birth parents return home to family members who did not support their decision and may be angry, judgmental, or outright rejecting. Even supportive family members may convey the message that the birth parents should not dwell on the pain of the past. Many people in this situation have not been able share their experiences with other birth parents, and few have met others who are actively engaged in ongoing open relationships.

Being in an ongoing relationship with the adoptive family can help a birth parent to establish a new sense of self. Meg, who was 19 years old when she gave birth, remembers:

> After the birth, I returned to the town where I had to continue to keep the adoption a secret. It was as though it didn't happen, like I wasn't a real person who had had a real child. It wasn't until I started to see my son's adoptive family that I began to feel better about who I was and what I had done.

Beth, a 21-year-old birth mother, says:

> When I went back to college, I didn't know who I was going to be or how I should act now that I had placed a baby for adoption. During the first year of contact, as I grew more comfortable with his family, I began to realize that I was somebody important: I had made this person and he would always be a part of me.

Once the initial decision has been made to stay in contact, it still may be difficult to carry it out. Some birth parents reported that the initial meetings with adoptive parents were wrought with anxiety and trepidation. Peggy had her first visit with the adoptive family when her birth son was one month old. She remembers many of the difficult feelings:

> I didn't know what it was going to be like. I was scared that my milk would come in if I was near him. I also didn't know how I would relate to them (the adoptive parents) now that they knew him better than I did. It felt a little like we were walking on eggshells that first visit. We were both trying so hard to be so nice to each other and make sure we didn't make any mistakes. It felt a little like a first date. But with each visit, it got easier.

It wasn't until I started to see my son's adoptive family that I began to feel better about who I was and what I had done.

Meg,
a 19-year-old
birth mother

Making Room in Our Hearts

Although openness can help a birth parent find a valuable role to play in the life of the child, it is no panacea for the grief and loss experienced by birth parents. Birth parents may indeed feel less guilty, less shamed, and more able to resolve grief issues in open relationships, but these benefits should not be used as a carrot to entice them toward an adoption decision. Grotevant and McRoy concluded that no matter what the type of adoption, from closed to fully open, some birth parents resolved their grief issues, while others did not.

In *Being a Birth Parent, Finding Our Place* (1999), Brenda Romanchik, an adoption educator and advocate for openness, asks us to remember:

> For birth mothers especially, the abruptness of the separation is like an amputation. Physically, as well as emotionally, there is a void in our lives where our baby once had been. We may hear our baby crying. We may feel like there is a hole inside that can never be filled. For many birth parents, it is the first experience of so profound a loss. Many are surprised by the intensity of the pain, anger, guilt and depression that are a normal part of the grieving process. Over the long term, we grieve the child, the teenager, and the adult our baby would have become had we raised him. That person will never be. It is a loss that is revisited again and again. (pages 10–11)

Gail, a birth mother with a son in open adoption since his birth 10 years ago, put it this way:

> I don't know what they mean by the word "resolve". It sounds like you are supposed to tie it up, and put it in a nice little box. I love seeing my child grow up in a wonderful family. I love that he knows who I am, but I would be lying if I said that it never hurts any more. Maybe hurt is the wrong word. It's not like I am grieving—it's just that adoption is bittersweet. In the best of all worlds, I wish this didn't have to happen, but seeing him grow and being part of his life has now become the best of all worlds to me.

Cathy is the birth mother of Lindsay, age 8. Her feelings illustrate some of the complexity of letting go and staying in touch:

> I didn't know what I was getting into when I decided to place my daughter for adoption, but I did hope that she and I could meet some-day. Her parents were such great people, and I could see the open relationship they had with their older daughter's birth mother. I saw Lindsay until she was 8 months old, and then I moved away and haven't seen her since. We talk and exchange letters and photos, but it is still hard for me. When people asked if I had children, I might

Over the long term, we grieve the child, the teenager, and the adult our baby would have become had we raised him. That person will never be. It is a loss that is revisited again and again.

— Brenda Romanchik, adoption educator and advocate

say one and feel guilty, or I would say none and feel guilty too. I was going through a lot of sadness and guilt about the whole thing, but knowing that Lindsay was in great hands and would get a good education helped me get through those hard times.

Eight years later, I still have a lot of feelings about this. I probably would start crying if I saw her now, and I'm not ready for that. I would never want to risk that any contact I might have with her might hurt her parents. *I am also a little afraid of having too much longing if I saw her.* I'm not sure I want to open that door again right now, but at the same time, I don't want any secrets or lies. My son is only 2 years old, but I have talked with him about his sister. I put Lindsay's picture in his baby book because she *is* his sister. I don't know what will happen in the future, but I know that they might have a relationship when they are grown up.

If birth parents want to continue to have contact with their child, they will need support and guidance to work through their own losses, or their grief may interfere with forming a healthy connection with the adoptive family. No matter how wonderful the birth of this child is to the adoptive family, we need to understand and validate the very different experience of the birth mother. Brenda Romanchik reminds us:

> We should not underestimate the magnitude of the suffering that many birth mothers go through, even if they are well prepared. You can never be totally prepared for grief. Adoptive parents want to see the joy of adoption, but they need to realize that relinquishment can be filled with sadness and anger. Birth parents don't get flowers, they don't get showers, and most of them return to families that don't want to talk about their loss. (interview, 2004)

Birth parents who have support from their adoption professionals to tackle these intense emotions are often able to come out the other side, realizing that while they have relinquished their role as parents, they have not given up their right to love and contribute to that child's life.

Keeping Agreements about Contact

One of the other major fears that birth parents have is that adoptive parents will renege on their contact agreements, or discontinue contact completely. Many birth parents feel that during the pregnancy, the potential adoptive parents pay very close attention to them, becoming good friends and advocates, but many are afraid that after the baby is born the adoptive parents may want to lessen contact. Facing the possibility of losing contact leaves birth parents feeling especially powerless. Adoptive parents need to

Adoptive parents want to see the joy of adoption, but they need to realize that relinquishment can be filled with sadness and anger. Birth parents don't get flowers, they don't get showers, and most of them return to families that don't want to talk about their loss.

— Brenda Romanchik, adoption educator and advocate

understand that they are not "doing a favor" to the birth parents by promising openness. Agreements about openness need to come from a mutual understanding of the benefits to the child.

The most important step birth and adoptive parents can take to lessen the likelihood of broken agreements, is to discuss their hopes and expectations for the relationship with the help of experienced open adoption professionals. Unexplored differences in expectations can lead to confusion, hurt, and fears of the relationship unraveling.

Lisa, a 21-year-old birth mother, remembers:

When my birth son was about 4 months old, the adoptive mom and I seemed to become irritated with each other. I think she was really frazzled, and didn't want me to see that, but at the time, I misunderstood and was freaked out that they might be pulling back. Then we started e-mailing each other, which added to the confusion. We finally got some help from our adoption agency, which clarified a lot. I just desperately wanted some assurance that I would have a role in his life. They had assumed that I would be in his life, but they just needed some space.

Another way to address concerns about ongoing contact, is to make a formal or informal agreement. Many of the families interviewed here felt comfortable speaking with each other about contact, and did not require anything more formal than a conversation. They felt that their agreements were part of a trusted covenant between them, one that did not require a written agreement. Others thought that writing down some of their basic understandings about visits would be helpful, especially in the beginning when everyone was trying to sort out their relationship.

Several states offer future contact agreements within the legal adoption process itself. California passed legislation in 2001 that allows for the filing of these agreements during the legal proceedings. The regulation mandates that birth and adoptive parents be informed about the right to have written agreements about contact. If both parties agree, open adoption agreements are written and included in the adoption proceedings. These contracts can be general or specific, and typically might include the frequency of visits or how to deal with holidays and birthdays. If these agreements are not kept, either party, after a good faith effort at mediation, may go to court to have the order enforced. Failure to follow the terms of these agreements will never set aside the adoption, but they create a venue for communication if one party reneges on agreements. These agreements are not meant to dictate how adoptive parents should respond to inappropriate behavior. If a birth parent were to show up for a meeting intoxicated and the adoptive

Don't worry about whose turn it is to call or write. Keep focused on the child. No matter what pain it will bring you, it is bound to be more painful for your child to not know you.

— Arlene, a birth mother

parents decided to temporally halt meetings, no court would interfere with that process.

Many agree that if written agreements do exist, they should serve as a covenant between parties more than as a legally binding obligation. Melina and Roszia (1993) have argued that legally mandated agreements go against the grain of what should be at the center of open adoption: trust, flexibility, and honesty. "We believe open adoptions are relationships more than agreements, and we are not in favor of the court system being used to negotiate relationships. The child's needs in open adoption are better met by a good relationship between birth and adoptive parents than by court mandated letter, phone calls or visits" (pages 211–212).

It is not only birth parents who have fears of interrupted or discontinued contact. Adoptive parents who are committed to openness also worry about the ability of birth parents to maintain their commitment to them and their child. They may be afraid of their child suffering another set of losses if they begin a relationship with the birth parents, only to lose it in the future. Many birth parents seem to go through a period of lessened contact, especially after they have felt assured that their child is secure in their new family. Adele, an adoptive mother, remembers that sinking feeling when her daughter's birth mother disappeared after the first year.

> I was so scared that she wouldn't come back. Although I needed some time to claim my daughter as my own, I didn't want to lose our relationship. She eventually resurfaced, and now that I have two kids with two different birth mothers, I can see a pattern of them needing some space after the first year or two. It was as though they had to get settled in their lives before they could come back and reconnect to our family.

There will be times in most open relationships when contact changes, just as in other familial relationships. It is important to remember that everyone who enters into an open adoption may not always be able to keep agreements, but these relationships are not static. An adoptive mother who feels extremely protective of her newly formed bond with a child, might need more space from a birth parent than either had anticipated. When she finds herself more secure in her role as a parent, she may establish more contact with the birth parents. A birth mother who finds herself in too much emotional pain to make a first birthday visit, might need to have an adoptive parent's permission to lessen contact until she is ready to have visits at other less emotionally loaded times. The families that seemed to do the best were those that understood that it was "normal" to have ups and downs in the degree of contact. They did not take that to mean that either of them was backing away from their overall commitment.

The families that seemed to do the best were those that understood that it was "normal" to have ups and downs in the degree of contact. They did not take that to mean that either of them was backing away from their overall commitment.

Claiming a Child as One's Own

For many adoptive parents, the fears about openness can often be understood as an overall concern about the ability to claim the child as their own. Without knowing other families who have successfully navigated open adoption, it is easy for adoptive parents to be anxious about these nagging questions: will I feel like my parenting is being judged if the birth parents are in the picture? I want to feel a special kind of bond between myself and my child, won't that be lessened if the birth mother is involved? Will the child feel more connected to his birth parents once he understands genetics and heredity?

Michelle was a new adoptive mother when she began to have conflicting feelings about contact with the birth mother. "I went from feeling totally connected to the expectant mother during those last six weeks of the pregnancy, and then shifted to feeling very threatened about my role as a new mother. Raising my son became the center of my life, and I didn't want the birth mother to take anything away from that." When the birth mother called six weeks after birth, requesting to see the adoptive family, Michelle was definitely not ready for contact, "I was surprised and overwhelmed by these feelings because no one had prepared me, or maybe I wasn't ready to hear it." The birth mother meanwhile, had her own fears that she wouldn't be able to participate as much as she wanted to in this child's life and needed to see the baby.

Michelle, her husband, and the birth mother decided to go through a series of counseling sessions with their agency. Michelle recalls, "Those sessions were very painful, but they were also very helpful. We all talked openly about our fears and how it was difficult to tell each other how we were feeling. We came out of those meetings much clearer about agreements about future contact. There was nothing written at the time, and no other families like ours to talk with, so the counseling sessions were invaluable." This family has been connecting to their son's birth mother for over 18 years and can now look back with a smile as they remember their initial confusion.

Adoptive parents need to know that *openness is an opportunity, not an obligation.* Just as birth parents need to choose to deal with their grief about the loss of their parenting role, adoptive parents need to choose openness— not because they have to, and not because they feel like "we won't get a child if we don't," but because they understand the benefits to themselves and their child. It is important that neither the birth nor the adoptive parents enter into arrangements where they feel pressured or mistrustful. The job of adoption professionals is to support the exploration of these concerns, and to separate the usual fears about openness from resistance to following through on commitments.

Adoptive parents need to choose openness— not because they have to, and not because they feel like "we won't get a child if we don't," but because they understand the benefits to themselves and their child.

The overall question about being able to fully claim the child as one's own usually includes other specific concerns: What if the birth parents are intrusive or invasive? What if they have inappropriate behaviors? Openness is sometimes seen as an open-door policy, where birth parents can walk right in and adoptive parents lose control over their own family. Of course there will be some birth parents who have trouble keeping agreements, and others who may not be very skilled in respecting boundaries. However, most of the adoptive parents reported that birth parents were particularly sensitive to their needs because of their own concerns about invading the adoptive family's space.

It is important to remember that relationships with birth parents will change over time, and adoptive parents can be partners in that process, not victims. Although adoptive parents are *partnering* with the birth family in creating an open relationship, they are not *partnering* in being parents.

Birth parents are not experts who need to be consulted. Adoptive parents will have the power and control to create the family norms that are right for their family.

Birth parents are not experts who need to be consulted. Adoptive parents will have the power and control to create the family norms that are right for their family.

Who Are the "Real" Parents?

Both birth and adoptive parents may have concerns about who are the "real" parents? *Everyone is real but there is only one set of parents.* Birth parents will need to face the losses of their parenting role, and adoptive parents will need to fully claim their role as the child's parents. However, society often upholds the primacy of the connection between birth parents and their offspring, but does not provide equal validation for the relationship between adoptive parents and their children. This may contribute to the sense of not quite being the "real" parents.

When my daughter was 7, we were driving home from school when she told me that someone in her class had said that I wasn't her "real" mom. I started to ask her what that meant to her, and how she felt about it while I was still driving. But at a certain point, I realized that this crucial conversation about who was "real" should not happen while the car was moving, at least not for me. I pulled over to the side of the road, and turned around saying,

We are all very real. Your birth mother was, and is, very real and she *really* didn't feel ready to be a mom yet when she was pregnant. And I am *really* your Mom as I have been loving you and taking care of you since the moment you were born, and will continue to be your Mom forever. And you are *really real*, and you are part of me, and your Dad, and also a part of your birth mom and your birth father, and you always will be. We are all real!

Making Room in Our Hearts

I could say this because I knew who I was, and I was absolutely certain about my emotional, physical, and spiritual claim as my daughter's parent.

It may be helpful to ask yourself, what makes a parent a parent? Most of us will answer that the daily tasks of loving, nurturing, protecting, guiding, supporting, disciplining, and educating our children make us parents. Parenting includes the hundreds of daily ways we help our children grow and develop into whole human beings. Melina and Roszia (1993) underline this point:

> There is a bond between children and their birth parents, but it isn't solely what accounts for the close feelings between parents and child. That feeling is a direct result of parenting: getting up in the middle of the night to feed your child, bandaging him after he scrapes his knee and comforting him when he is in emotional pain. Regardless of the bond that exists at birth, a child is going to form his close parent–child attachment with the adoptive parents because he can depend on them to meet his needs on a day-to-day basis. The birth parent who writes, calls, visits, or even cares for the child in the parent's absence, is not going to interfere with that attachment process. (page 16)

Brenda Romanchik adds an important point about the difference between claiming a child and owning a child. "All adopted children need to be claimed by their adoptive parents. But claiming should not be confused with ownership. Birth parents also need to claim this child, because they too have the right to identify their role in creating this child's life." (Interview, 2004) The connection with birth parents does not lessen the emotional and legal rights of the adoptive family to fully claim their role as the child's parents.

Will the Child Be Confused?

Another concern that both birth and adoptive parents may have is that children will be confused, or that they might have mixed feelings of loyalty. There is often a lurking fear in the back of adoptive mothers' minds that the primacy of the relationship with the birth mother, will at some point, trump her role as the Mom. Some adoptive parents have fears that during the teens, the child will turn to them and scream, "I hate you and I want to go and live with my birth parents!" Other parents joke that during the teens, they would *like* them to go live somewhere else! On other occasions, children might use the word *real* to describe their birth parents. They might say things in anger, like Kayla did to her mother when she was demanding that she complete her chores. "Well, I don't know why I have to do all this or listen to you. Actually, you are not even *really* my mother."

Regardless of the bond that exists at birth, a child is going to form his close parent–child attachment with the adoptive parents because he can depend on them to meet his needs on a day-to-day basis.

— Lois Melina and Sharon Kaplan Roszia

Once at a young age, my daughter was having a very difficult time completing the task of brushing her teeth, and I was starting to talk about consequences. She whined back at me, "If I was with my birth mother, she wouldn't make me brush my teeth!" I took a breath, and told her in a relatively calm voice, "Your birth mom was not ready to be a mom to anyone, but some day if she is, she will probably make sure that her children brush their teeth. And right now, I am your Mom, and it is my job to make sure you take good care of your body, so brush your teeth!" These comments and others like them don't indicate that the child or teen is confused. They indicate that kids are using the time-honored device of attempting to divide and conquer in order to get their way. Should adopted children be any less sophisticated at these maneuvers than other children are? Comments like this can only work if adoptive parents are feeling doubts that may be detected by the special radar equipment of children and teens. Adoptive parents need to address their own losses so these areas of vulnerability do not affect their ability to feel confident in their role as parents.

Each of the teens and young adults interviewed for this book were absolutely clear about the different roles of their parents and their birth parents. One adopted teenager who had frequent contact with his birth parents reported: "It's the parents who are always there and will always be there no matter what. My birth parents made me, but these people raised me and that's a big difference." Another said, "I don't think we should even call them parents because they aren't parents at all. I love my birth mom and I am totally glad she is in my life, but she is definitely not my parent."

It may be difficult, it not impossible, for people who have not experienced open adoption to understand how adopted persons seem to effortlessly balance multiple parental figures unless we remember that birth parents *are not parental figures*. Children understand the differences between a close aunt whom they might see frequently, or a godmother who is an integral part of their life, and their parents, and the same is true of birth parents. Children may love them, they may have a special place in the life of their family, but they are *not* parents. We need to remember that if the adults involved are not confused or conflicted about their roles, the children are not likely to be confused either.

Keeping the Dialogue Open

The fears and concerns that birth and adoptive parents have about openness need to be explored during the adoption process, and at any point they arise, whether it is after the placement, or when the child is 5 or 10 years old. Adoptive and birth parents need to ask their professionals to assist them as they work together to explore their hopes, dreams, and expectations. These are some of the questions that may be helpful to consider:

It's the parents who are always there, and will always be there no matter what. My birth parents made me, but these people raised me and that's a big difference.

— An adopted teenager

Making Room in Our Hearts

- What are some of the benefits of openness to the child and to the birth and adoptive parents?
- What are each of their concerns about this relationship? What are they most afraid of happening? What could they do to address this fear?
- How would they prefer to deal with conflict or disagreements that might come up? If it is hard to talk about the relationship with each other, where might they go for support?
- What kinds of contact do they each think they might want? Who will initiate the contact and how? How would they like to proceed if contact is disrupted or disconnected by either party?
- How will adoptive and birth parents keep each other updated if there are moves or changes in contact information?
- Look down the road toward the time when the child is 5, 10, or in the teen years. What kind of relationship would the birth and adoptive parents like to have developed with each other and with the child?

A Team Pulling in the Same Direction

The following profile is unusual in that the adoptive mother, Mary Martin Mason, and the birth mother Lisa, were themselves adopted. Mary has the perspective of having experienced open adoption in her own childhood. After her mother died when she was 2, her father arranged for her to be placed in a family that he knew would allow her to maintain contact with her two brothers who stayed with her father. Mary is an open adoption educator and advocate and is also the Adoption Information Clearinghouse Coordinator for the Minnesota Adoption Support and Preservation Project.

Mary Martin Mason, Adoptive Mother of Josh

People growing up in their families of origin take for granted the thousands of ways that they fit in. They have hundreds of stories told to them their whole lives about who they are like, and who they look like that root them in their tribe. I wanted that for my son and, when Josh was 5, we decided to open up the adoption with our agency's help. That first meeting was a little scary for all of us, but Josh, even at age 5, was clear about his own needs. When we told him that Lisa, myself, and his dad would be meeting separately, he put his hands on his hips and said in no uncertain terms, "That's not fair. She is my real mom, and I should get to meet her too." Not only was "real mom" not politically correct, it was a term never used in our family. We just knew it meant that Josh understood the importance of the woman who had given birth to him.

When Josh was 10, he turned a corner in his relationship with his birth mother. She was expected to come for a Christmas visit, and she

From left to right: Mary Martin Mason, Josh Mason, and Lisa Widman. Mary is the adoptive mother of Josh and Lisa is his birth mother.

had to cancel at the last minute. When he discovered that she wasn't coming, his disappointment was huge, and that helped us all understand how much he needed her in his life. Throughout his teens, they continued to deepen their connection, and they occasionally spent weekends together. Josh and Lisa are incredibly alike in so many ways, and she has provided a reality check for him as he has grown up.

As a professional, I try to help birth and adoptive parents understand openness by standing in the child's shoes. What would it feel like to have this big hole inside that leaves you feeling insecure? We need to remember that our children grow up, and will live much of their lives without us, but will carry their sense of identity with them forever. Adults make these relationships complicated when they do not have to be. Open adoption is not co-parenting, but it is a sharing of the history and the love for our children.

Lisa Widman, Birth Mother of Josh, Speaking at Age 40

When I found myself pregnant in my second year of college, I immediately considered adoption, but I knew I couldn't live with a closed one. Being adopted myself, I had always wondered who I looked like, as I felt physically and emotionally different from everyone else in my family. I thought that someone did not want me, and I spent my childhood trying to figure out why. I remember feeling very confused: was I supposed to be like my mother and father, or was I supposed to be like the people who didn't want me? I scanned crowds trying to find people who might be my birth parents. I would fantasize about who they were and imagine all sorts of possibilities. By age 12, I had developed two separate identities. On the outside, I looked like I fit in, but on the inside, I had nothing to fill out the picture of who I really was.

I never told my parents how confused I felt. All they saw was my intense fondness for strangers. Throughout my teens, I continued to try on different hats because I had really no idea in whose footsteps I was supposed to follow. This had nothing to do with my adoptive parents, because I loved them and feel totally loved by them. They had always told me about adoption in the most positive light, but they had almost no information about my origins. The painful feelings about my own adoption definitely influenced my decision when I found myself pregnant. Not only was I not ready to parent, but also I had fears about being *able* to parent, given that I felt so unsure about my own identity.

The intensity of my grief after my son was born was overwhelming. I wanted Josh, as I had named him, to go home with his parents and to be able to meet them after he was settled in his new home, but the agency wouldn't allow that. Back in 1986, open adoption in Minnesota meant that you could write a letter with no identifying information, and the agency would send it to the adoptive parents. Within two weeks after placement, I was overjoyed when I received a birth announcement, and read that they had named him Josh, not even knowing that it was the same name I had given him. We continued communicating through the agency, and Mary, the adoptive mom, told me that she had written a book on infertility. Soon after, I was watching TV, and saw a woman talking about infertility and I just knew it was she.

When Josh was 5, Mary wrote me and said they were ready to meet. I was terrified that I would be thrown back into the hurt of the pregnancy and the relinquishment, but Mary and Doug were so appreciative and respectful that I felt reassured. Mary was also adopted, and having that similarity made a big difference to me. We didn't talk about what our relationship would look like in the future; it just evolved into contact every three to four months.

When Josh was 8, I was diagnosed with cancer, and it threw me into a very painful period. All of my identity issues were magnified by the losses that cancer brought to my life, including not being able to have any other children. The grief brought back the pain of having lost Josh

> *By age 12, I had developed two separate identities. On the outside, I looked like I fit in, but on the inside, I had nothing to fill out the picture of who I really was.*
>
> — Lisa, a birth mother who is also an adoptee

as a baby, and I had to take space from my relationship with his family. I knew that I was grieving for the loss of Josh as a baby, not for the loss of Josh as an 8-year-old. Many birth mothers will tell you that: they are grieving for the baby that they could not parent. I felt that I couldn't be good at open adoption when I was in so much pain. Mary was wonderful through all of this. When I needed to fade in and out, she let me know that she understood, but would be there when I returned.

There was a turning point when Josh was around 10, and he wanted every detail of the story about why I had made an adoption decision. It seemed like I was becoming a more important part of his life, so I honored that by making a decision that I wasn't going to pull away anymore. Sure, teen years can be hard, but we were clear about boundaries. If I am concerned about something that Josh tells me, I feel obligated to share that with his parents. Mary is his mother, not me. Sometimes I can help him through hard times because he and I are so very much alike in our temperament. It's important to remember that as your kids get older, they are more of a part of the open adoption equation. Josh expresses his needs and makes some of his own decisions about contact.

I decided to search for my own birth family, and Josh and I traveled to meet them for the first time when he when he was 13 years old. We met my birth mother and maternal grandmother, and it was amazing to meet people who looked and acted like us. My birth mother was faced with the loss of what we had not shared, and was grieving for the baby *she* had lost 35 years before. It was as if it had happened to her yesterday. Josh and I came to the conclusion that it is much more difficult to meet your birth family as an adult than as a child.

My advice to birth and adoptive parents would be the same: kids deserve to know who they are and where they come from. It can be painful and complicated in the beginning, but it gets easier. Adoptive parents need to remember that birth parents don't want to parent. We made a choice, and it was not made lightly. We can provide guidance, be a confidante, a close and special friend, but we are not parents.

> *Adoptive parents need to remember that birth parents don't want to parent. We made a choice, and it was not made lightly. We can provide guidance, be a confidante, a close and special friend, but we are not parents.*
>
> — Lisa, a birth mother

Josh Mason, Age 21

The greatest advantage of open adoption is that I have someone I can identify with. There are so many similarities in our personalities between my birth mother and myself. It is uncanny how often we think alike, and have mannerisms that are similar. It makes me feel like I am not some random case. I love my family, but I am just different from them. If I didn't know my birth mother, I think I would feel like an oddball. Knowing my birth mother has helped me feel more normal growing up. It is really refreshing to be with Lisa's family and see people a little more like me.

People always ask me when I speak at conferences, "Doesn't this make you confused?" And I always respond: "Kids aren't stupid. I think I would be confused if my birth mother was not in my life. There would be so many unanswered questions." I just started an accounting class and have found, much to my surprise, that I really love working with numbers. When I went with Lisa to be reunited with her birth mother and birth grandmother, I learned that they had both worked as accountants. Seeing where parts of me come from is really important to me. Sure, it probably takes a lot more work and investment of emotions, but I definitely think there is a lot to be gained. I cannot imagine life without having this connection.

My parents, especially my Mom, have always been great at making this work for all of us. I never experienced competition between them—it felt like they were a team pulling in the same direction. Some of what makes it work is that they have been really honest with each other. That is one of the keys—being brutally honest if you need to be, even if the truth isn't that great. It is the child's truth, and shouldn't be hidden from them.

A lot of people don't get open adoption at first, but most of my friends did. We all saw other adopted kids from the closed system, and you could see that it was harder. I think openness lessens some of the pain. I know my birth mother isn't in some tent somewhere along the side of the road. It is really important to know your birth family is OK. Knowing her has helped me understand and support her decision, because I know it was the best she could have done at the time.

Open adoption isn't confusing because there is nothing to be confused about. My birth mother is not another parent. The word parent doesn't even come to mind. My parents are my center of gravity. They have created a world for me, and they have widened that world to include everything in my life. My identity has its roots in my birth family but I have never even thought I would like to go and live with Lisa as a parent. Your parents are your parents. My birth mother is really important to me—she is like a special aunt, but she is not my parent. My advice to adoptive and birth parents would be to put yourself in our shoes. If it were you, you would probably want to know all of who you are.

My birth mother is not another parent. The word parent doesn't even come to mind. My parents are my center of gravity. They have created a world for me, and they have widened that world to include everything in my life.

— Josh Martin Mason

CHAPTER 4

"This Baby Belongs To Herself, and the More People Who Love Her, the Better"

For people in the beginning stages of adoption, the concept of openness may raise more questions than answers. Pre-adoptive parents often address their concerns gradually by attending workshops and reading books. Not so for Allison and Jeff of northern California. While still in the throes of considering infertility treatments, they attended an adoption orientation that included a panel of birth mothers and adoptive parents who talked movingly about their experiences with both open and closed adoption. As they left the room, they had a shared epiphany of sorts. They looked at each other and both concluded, "Why do an IVF? Let's just do an open adoption!"

The birth mothers they had listened to that night had made a strong impression. One birth mother who had relinquished her child 15 years earlier in a closed adoption, was still experiencing grief. The contrast between the birth mother who did not know if her child was alive, and the one in an open adoption was vivid. Allison remembers, "Open adoption seemed much more humane. The idea that the birth parents were choosing you, made it so much easier to consider." Jeff felt that the concepts underlying openness were consistent with his own beliefs: "I felt that the biological connections were very important and to arbitrarily sever them by legal means would not be in the best interest of the child."

Even though Jeff and Allison were united in their desire for an open adoption, they still felt as though they were jumping off a cliff. Jeff saw the connection between children and their birth parents as "a fundamental part of nature," even though he was aware that openness was a relatively new social experiment. "In opening their lives to their child's birth parents, I could see that other adoptive families did not feel threatened, and were not devaluing their role as parents. That gave me the courage to move forward." Realizing this, their initial adoption outreach letter made it clear that they desired ongoing contact with a birth family.

Six months later, they met Jody, who was three months pregnant. Although they discussed openness, they never talked about what their future relationship would look like when the child was older. Allison recalls:

> We weren't really looking at the future at all. We liked each other and knew we wanted to be connected for ourselves and for the child, but we just trusted that it would evolve. It's sort of like falling in love and getting married. You don't talk about what it will be like to share a mortgage or go through menopause or old age together. You just do it. It is the same when you have a baby. We didn't consider what the relationship would be like when the child was 15.

Having met in the first trimester, Allison, Jeff, and Jody had plenty of opportunity to get to know one another. Their time together included some of the rocky periods of the pregnancy. Allison remembers, "One of Jody's early letters asked us what we would do if the baby had a disability. Would we back out of the adoption? As we began to deal with some of our mutual fears, we were able to deepen our trust of each other."

After the birth, the baby girl, who was named Zoe, had a minor medical problem that required her to stay in the hospital for a few days. For some adoptive parents, the period when the child is still in the hospital may provoke tension about who exactly the child *belongs to*, but Allison says there were some principles that she felt guided by during this time. "I felt like the baby belonged to herself. This child does not belong to either of us—she is her own person. I deeply believed that the more people who loved this baby, the better."

Concern about how Jody was doing was uppermost in Allison's mind. Two days after the birth, she sat in a hallway outside the room where Jody was signing the relinquishment papers, and Allison found herself starting to sob. "The full realization that I was becoming a mother was hitting me, but mostly I was tuned into what Jody must have been going through. The language in the relinquishment process is so brutal—that a birth mother is giving up all rights *forever* for the child she has just given birth to." Allison could empathize with the pain that Jody was going through because she had the chance to experience her not as a stereotypical birth mother, but as a real person, a flesh-and-blood woman who was making one of the most difficult decisions of her life.

In opening their lives to their child's birth parents, I could see that other adoptive families did not feel threatened, and were not devaluing their role as parents. That gave me the courage to move forward.

— Jeff, an adoptive father

Making Room in Our Hearts

From left to right: Jody, Zoe, and Allison. Jody is the birth mother of Zoe and Allison is the adoptive mother.

Since Allison, Jeff, and Jody had developed a pattern of contact, they thought they would do more of the same after the baby was born. The only time there was an explicit mention of ongoing contact was at the entrustment ceremony. Entrustment ceremonies are rituals to acknowledge that birth parents are relinquishing their role as parents, and placing their trust in an adoptive family to provide a loving and permanent home. These ceremonies can be as simple or complex as the families' desire, and are best when both birth and adoptive parents are the architects. At this one, a candle was passed around the circle and each person made a wish for the baby. Jody's father, the birth grandfather, said to Jeff and Allison: "I really do hope we see you again." Allison remembers thinking, "He doesn't have to worry. I know they are part of my family and we are now part of theirs. I was certain that we would fulfill our promise to stay connected."

The circle of connection widened as Allison's parents welcomed this child into their lives. Initially, they had thought that open adoption was a little "too much," but with education, Allison's mother felt that having contact simply made sense. When Jody made the first visit to the adoptive family at their home, Allison's parents wanted to meet her. Allison recalls, "After an initial period of adjustment, my parents have developed a close and fond relationship with Jody. My father has become an open adoption advocate and tells everyone about how great it is."

Jeff's parents love and adore their two grandchildren, but they have not embraced open adoption. They don't talk about the birth parents and are

> *I felt like the baby belonged to herself. This child does not belong to either of us—she is her own person. I deeply believed that the more people who loved this baby, the better.*
>
> — Allison, an adoptive mother

reluctant to hear how the visits have gone. Allison wistfully remarks, "They are of the old school and feel strongly that this is wrong for the child, wrong for the birth mother, and wrong for us." Jeff's father, an obstetrician, had assisted in adoptions under the closed system. Based on his experience, he believes that continued contact causes undue pain for the birth mother. Jeff understands his parents' reluctance and accepts their position. "They have formed a strong attachment to our kids, but they don't agree with our decision about openness. We consider our children's birth mothers to be extended members of our family and they do not, so we have to live with that."

Allison and Jeff always wanted more than one child, and eventually made contact with a woman named Molly, who was 16 at the time and clear about wanting an open adoption. Molly had felt deceived by the first couple she had worked with who initially had agreed to some openness, but later voiced discomfort with ongoing contact. Turning to new adoptive parents late in her pregnancy, Molly wanted to be certain they would follow through with their agreements. In this case, she had the advantage of knowing the kind of relationship Allison and Jeff had developed with their first child's birth mother.

Molly visited Allison and Jeff when her birth son, Leo, was 5 months old and wanted to visit again on his birthday, thus starting a tradition of annual birthday visits. When Allison was asked if she ever felt this might lessen her own celebration of Leo's birthday, she replied with certainty: "Both of my kids' birth mothers are very considerate. I never feel like I am obligated to have a visit. It's more like they are family and we want them to visit." Jeff agrees, "It is a little difficult logistically to have two extended families, but it always feels right."

Over the past few years, they have left their kids with their respective birth mothers for a few days so that Allison and Jeff could have some time for themselves. Allison says, "For me this is total self-interest. I don't know anyone who will take care of them as willingly and as lovingly as their birth parents, and I welcome the chance to have them be with each other while we get away."

As for the frequent question that people have about open adoption as to whether the kids will be confused about who their "real" parents are, Jeff feels strongly about this:

> In Zoe's case, she has no question about who her parents are, and she knows that she came from Jody's tummy. Because she witnessed her brother Leo's adoption, I think it has helped her understand what her own adoption story is about. I think the kids look to us to see what level of comfort we have. It seems really natural to them because it seems really natural to us.

Both of my kids' birth mothers are very considerate. I never feel like I am obligated to have a visit. It's more like they are family and we want them to visit.

— Allison, an adoptive mother

Making Room in Our Hearts

From top to bottom: Molly, Leo, and Zoe. Molly is Leo's birth mother. Leo and Zoe are siblings.

Class differences are almost always a part of adoption. Lack of financial resources frequently influence the decisions made when birth parents are confronted with an unexpected pregnancy. Adoptive parents are usually more privileged and often have significantly more financial resources than birth parents. These differences can create problems that need clarification and negotiation as the relationships develop. For this family, class issues presented themselves differently. Both Jeff and Allison felt somewhat scrutinized in the early stages by Molly's upper-middle-class mother who seemed to want to be assured of the level of resources that would be committed to raising Leo. Allison recalls, "I sometimes felt a little defensive about whether I was meeting her standards, but I have also never felt like she would intrude in any way." Allison and Jeff understood that these were normal concerns of a grandparent for her first grandchild, and although it was occasionally irritating, they were able to put it aside. They knew that roles and boundaries would become clearer to everyone as the relationships progressed, and they have found this to be true.

Because Molly and Jody live in the same state, it makes Allison and Jeff's visits to the two birth families easier. Allison said, "When we visit, we see both families separately, but there is some crossover, especially at the airport where they have all come together to see us off." Jeff adds that:

> They are very different people. Jody was older and much more independent when she became pregnant, and has always been very clear about how much contact she wanted. Molly was in high school and was influenced by her mother's decisions about the pregnancy. She seemed to have more ambivalence about the whole process in the early stages, but she keeps the connection and has matured greatly over the past several years.

Both birth mothers have acknowledged to Allison and Jeff that it was hard in the beginning, but contact became less painful as time went on. Allison's close ties to Jody helped them talk freely about the emotional challenges of relinquishing a child for adoption. "I always asked how it was going for her, and how she was doing with the separation. It felt totally natural to talk about how hard it has been for her at times."

Allison and Jeff were aware of the developmental stages that allowed Zoe to understand more of the complexities of adoption, both for herself and for her birth mother. During a summer trip when she was 8 years old, Zoe met her half-sibling, a new baby girl born to Jody and her husband. Although there was some concern about how she might experience this new addition to her birth mother's family, she was thrilled to be a part of the baby's life. As Allison says, "She takes her cues from us and since we were so excited, I think she felt pretty good about it. We didn't get hung up on what we would call the baby, or how we would label the relationship. No one made a big deal about Jody deciding that she was ready to parent this baby, but was not ready to parent Zoe." Jeff and Allison both feel strongly that "We don't know how it will all work out, but we know that our daughter will know she *is* loved, and *was* loved even though her birth mother was not ready to parent her."

> *We don't know how it will all work out, but we know that our daughter will know she is loved, and was loved even though her birth mother was not ready to parent her.*
>
> — Allison, an adoptive mother

The Adoptive Grandparents

Allison's parents, Abe and Natalie, supported the adoption, but had to stretch a little to understand open adoption. Natalie remembers it well:

> I think it came together for me after the birth. Jody got on the phone and wanted to talk to me. From that point on, my comfort level with her was like family. I have an independent relationship with Jody and Molly, and I see a lot of them in their birth children. I try to explain to my friends that they are like aunts or cousins, but it is hard to describe. One of my reservations at first was a little jealousy. Will they claim these kids more? Will these kids love their birth family more? A lot of contact has put that at ease.

46   Making Room in Our Hearts

From left to right: Jeff holding Julia, Abe, Jody, Allison, Leo, Zoe, and Natalie. Allison and Jeff are the adoptive parents of Zoe and Leo. Jody is the birth mother of Zoe and mother to Julia. Natalie and Abe are the adoptive grandparents of Zoe and Leo.

Abe recalls, "Once when Jody was visiting the first year, she was holding Zoe, who began to cry. Jody then handed Zoe to Allison and said, 'Here Zoe, go to your mother.' That allayed our anxieties about the birth mother making a claim that would somehow lessen our roles as parents and grandparents." There was another moment that was important to Natalie: "Once Molly's mother came with her for a visit. As we left the house, her mom turned to me and said, 'I am so happy Leo has you as his grandparent.' I have to give her a lot of credit that she was able to accept and welcome me as her first grandson's grandmother."

When I asked what it has been like to see the birth parents reflected in their grandchildren's personalities, and not their own, this was Abe's reply: "I feel that Leo is especially close to me. I know he is biologically connected to his birth parents, but I think Leo feels that he is *my grandson*." At which point his wife, Natalie, interjects: "*because he is*." Abe continues, "I feel welcome to share him with others, but I know that he belongs in this family." It was clear talking to Abe and Natalie that they have truly claimed these children as their own grandchildren, and that openness has not challenged that claim, in fact, it has enhanced it.

One of the surprises that Natalie and Abe were pleased to report was that both birth families have extended themselves to Leo and Zoe and see them as siblings. Natalie remarks, "I didn't think that would happen. They talk about both kids together as family, not just focusing on their own birth child. They treat Zoe and Leo as exactly who they are in this family: brother and sister." Jody and Molly both agree that Allison and Jeff have been so inclusive of them that they felt it was easy to be inclusive of the entire adoptive family. This gets at the very heart of open adoption: the ability to see and experience the concept of family through a different lens.

A Glimpse into What Might Have Been

A summer visit to both birth families when Zoe was 8 and Leo was 4 brought up many feelings for Allison. This was the first time that the children stayed with their respective birth parents for several days. The similarities between the children's temperaments and their families of origin were apparent.

> I could see how much Zoe's personality was similar to others in her tribe, not just her birth mother, but the whole clan. They are solidly working class, and not as achievement-oriented as Jeff and I. Her life with them would not have included the same kind of pressure she gets from us. Her life with us is better in terms of material resources and exposure to all sorts of things, but I can also see her strong similarity to her tribe. I could see what she has gained, but I can also see what she has lost.

> Even with Leo, similar feelings came up. It was hard for me not to notice what he would have had if he had stayed with his birth family. It isn't that I question open adoption. I am glad we are connected, but am also glad that we live far enough away to have our separate lives.

Many birth and adoptive parents can see the benefits of open adoption, and want to offer that to their child, but they need to know their own limits.

Allison knows that the geographical distance between the families allows for annual contact, but lessens the opportunities for entanglement with each other's lives. Many birth and adoptive parents can see the benefits of open adoption, and want to offer that to their child, but they need to know their own limits.

Allison is courageously voicing some of the complex feelings that go with adoption. What would my children's lives have been like if they had stayed with their birth parents? How will my children feel about me as they grow up and see that they are more similar in some ways to their birth family? Parents in open adoption are able to give their children the sense of themselves as connected to both worlds, while growing up in one family. At times, this may bring a birth or adoptive parent face to face with some of the losses in adoption, but being aware of these losses is part of what makes a good parent for an adopted child. This terrain is similar to what the adopted child will have to walk as he builds his sense of self. Feeling the strong connection between her children and their birth families, Allison is able to better understand the tasks her children will face as they weave their identities from two different families into one whole person.

Jody, Birth Mother of Zoe

Jody began considering adoption as soon as she discovered that she was pregnant and was no longer involved with the birth father. "I didn't want to make a child suffer because I made a big mistake. I grew up on welfare and I knew I didn't want that for my kid, and I wasn't ready to be a single parent." Something clicked when Jody's doctor gave her Allison and Jeff's adoption letter. The couple's desire to have ongoing contact opened a door that Jody had not realized could be possible. She felt that the adoption decision would be much easier knowing that she could stay in touch with her child's new family.

> I knew that I was not going to be able to go through an entire pregnancy, and then give this child to someone I did not know. Allison and Jeff were so generous and we communicated so well, I felt that we would be able to figure it out, no matter what the future held. I began to feel more trusting that we would continue contact, but this was my Mom and Dad's first grandchild and it was very hard for them. I think my Dad understood more after the delivery when he saw how close I was with Allison and Jeff.

> After the birth, I had to get away. I needed some space away from the whole event. Those first few months were really hard, but getting pictures and hearing how Zoe was thriving made it a little easier. I felt better after talking with Allison because she didn't shy away from asking me how I was doing.

Some adoptive parents may not ask a birth mother how she is doing, fearing that if she talks about her grief, she may not follow through on her decision. It was clear that Allison had established a caring emotional bond to Jody as a person, not just because she had given her a baby.

By the time Allison, Jeff, and Zoe made their first visit to see Jody, things had changed. Jody's parents were more comfortable with the adoption and appreciative of openness. "My grandmother was so happy to meet them. This was her first great-grandchild, and it meant a lot to be able to see Zoe. Although my Mom and Dad have decided to keep some distance, they are glad that I have the contact I do." As she moved beyond the first few years, things got a little easier for Jody. "It was hard saying good-bye when Zoe was a baby, but now I have had many years of saying good-bye and saying hello. I know that I am always going to be able to see her again, and that makes it easier. In the beginning, I was mostly connected to Allison and Jeff, but now I have a relationship with Zoe and Leo, both of whom feel like part of my extended family."

It was hard saying good-bye when Zoe was a baby, but now I have had many years of saying good-bye and saying hello. I know that I am always going to be able to see her again, and that makes it easier.

— Jody, a birth mother

"This Baby Belongs To Herself, and the More People Who Love Her, the Better"

Several weeks after Jody gave birth to Zoe, she met her current husband. "At first he was reluctant to go along with the adoption. He felt that Zoe should be ours, and it was hard for him to accept. We went through some rough times because of it, but he has grown along with the contact." Six years later, Jody became pregnant again:

> This pregnancy was so different. The last time I felt so closed down. I didn't want to open myself up to the feelings because I knew I was choosing adoption, but this time, I was ready. I had a husband and a father for my child, and that is what I always wanted. I know it will be a challenge for Zoe to understand why I kept this child, but was unable to keep her. Allison and Jeff have prepared her as much as possible, and I know that she feels so loved by all of us, she will be able to understand.

And understand she did. Zoe knows that she has a very special relationship to Jody's new baby, although she seemed somewhat reluctant to have that relationship codified by language. Jody remarks:

> Zoe didn't want to be called the baby's sister, as though it would not be respectful to her relationship with her own family. It seems important to know who is who, and we all need a little bit of boundaries. I have to admit—it still is a little difficult to define these relationships. But if we don't define them too much, and just focus on being in the relationship, we do okay. As she grows older, Zoe reminds me so much of my family. She has some of the same personality quirks and expressions. It really makes me smile to see myself and my own family in her. She really is a part of me.

When asked how she sees open adoption now that her birth daughter is almost 12 years old, Jody says:

> Once that trust was established, we could deal with anything. Allison and Jeff have kept in contact just as they said they would: visits once a year and calls and photos about every three months—which is just enough. I have gotten some things that I did not expect from open adoption. Allison and Jeff have been models for me, like the way they read to their kids all the time, and I want to do that for my children. I would be lying though, if I didn't say there were some times that are hard. It is hard to not be able to see Zoe play soccer or pick her up from school. You know, daily life. Now that I have another child, I am especially aware of how I didn't get to do things with Zoe. But I wanted more for her than I was able to give her at the time. Yes, it is hard at times, but the benefits outweigh the pain.

Now that I have another child, I am especially aware of how I didn't get to do things with Zoe. But I wanted more for her than I was able to give her at the time. Yes, it is hard at times, but the benefits outweigh the pain.

— Jody,
birth mother
of Zoe

From left to right: Jeff, Allison, Jody, Molly's sister, Leo and Molly. Jeff and Allison are the adoptive parents of Leo and Molly is his birth mother. (Jody is the birth mother of Zoe, not pictured here)

Molly, Birth Mother of Leo

At 16 years old and about to enter her junior year in high school, Molly discovered that she was pregnant. She wasn't opposed to abortion on political or religious grounds, but she knew that it was not the right decision for her. As Molly perused "Dear Birth Mother" letters, she had so many concerns: "I knew that I had to feel connected to whoever would raise my child in order for me to let go of the baby. I also needed to know what it would be like for a child growing up in that family." Not knowing how to proceed, she told her mother when she was two months pregnant, and her divorced parents decided that she should move in with her father who lived an hour away:

> My parents are pretty conservative. After all, this is the Midwest. They were worried about their friends finding out, and were horrified about my younger brother and sister knowing the truth. They thought that it would be best if I kept the entire thing hidden and enrolled in a private Catholic school for girls. It was clear that I had no choice other than to do what they thought was right. Actually, the school turned out to be one of the few places I didn't feel judged and didn't have to hide my pregnancy.

Molly told the birth father when she was two months pregnant, but he then moved away and she was unable to locate him:

"This Baby Belongs To Herself, and the More People Who Love Her, the Better"   51

I was already feeling guilty about the pregnancy and having to be hidden away. His disappearing just compounded the shame. I felt like things had not changed much since the 1950s so far as my choices were concerned. I couldn't see my friends because the pregnancy was becoming too obvious. I couldn't call them because it was too hard to talk while keeping such a big part of my life a secret. Every day I felt guilty, isolated, and ashamed.

When she was seven months pregnant, her social worker began to discuss open adoption, but Molly remembers it being described as "a last ditch effort," with conflicts between birth and adoptive parents. Molly felt that the social worker conveyed her own fears about openness, trying to convince her that it would be less painful to close the door after the birth, but Molly did not want to close the door. As her pregnancy progressed, she became more anxious about the outcome and spent hours trying to work out different scenarios in her mind. "If someone would have just told me about open adoption, or turned me on to a book, or let me talk to another birth mom, everything would have been so different. The whole experience would have been so much less chaotic and overwhelming."

Molly was impressed when she received Allison and Jeff's letter, and read that they already had one adoption that was open. After having endured the shame of being hidden away for seven months, the idea that she could be involved with the adoptive family felt liberating. "Allison and Jeff sent me books about open adoption which were a godsend. Even my mom was relieved to be able to continue some involvement. I really couldn't have settled for less. Open adoption made it easier for me to let go of my parenting role."

Molly knows there are no rules in open adoption, which has occasionally left her feeling uncertain. Being in a relationship with a family that already has strong ties to another birth mother has had an effect on her.

In the beginning, I wanted to know exactly what the arrangements were with Jody, Zoe's birth mom, in order to know if I was doing the right thing. I preferred to not have a huge difference in the amount of contact that Zoe and Leo each has with their birth mothers. I was also more uncertain, and I wished there were clearer boundaries, but I know now that I am setting my own boundaries. Although it was a little difficult at times to see differences in parenting styles between how Allison and Jeff and I might do things, I feel great about Leo's family and knew that he was in a wonderful home with great parents!

When I first interviewed Molly, it had been five years since she had placed Leo for adoption, and the shame of that experience was still vivid in her

If someone would have just told me about open adoption, or turned me on to a book, or let me talk to another birth mom, everything would have been so different. The whole experience would have been so much less chaotic and over-whelming.

— Molly, birth mother of Leo

Making Room in Our Hearts

mind. "I tell this story, but it doesn't seem quite real to me, almost as though it is a fairy tale. I am not sure that I will have another child because I'm afraid it would bring back too many painful memories. I would be afraid of feeling the loss of what I did not have with my first pregnancy. I felt so alone, and ashamed and guilty. No one should have to feel like that."

Molly strongly that there should be more support for pregnant teens felt:

I had no support group and no other birth mothers to talk to. The social workers tried to be nice, but they talked to me as though I was stupid. They seemed to think that I had gotten myself into this mess, so I could not play any role in getting myself out of it. I wish that I could have been presented with options. No one, at any point, ever mentioned to me the possibility that I could keep this child and how I might do that. It's not that I was ready to parent, but no one even gave me the right to consider that possibility. When it came time to do all the legal papers, people asked me if I had been coerced in any way to relinquish, but no one ever really explored if I needed help in order to keep the baby.

Disclosure about the adoption was an ongoing issue for Molly and her family for several years. Her brother and sister, who were 13 and 11 at the time of the pregnancy, were not told about the adoption until Leo was 4 years old. Molly recalls, "Once when Allison and Jeff were visiting my family with Leo, we decided to tell my siblings that Leo was the son of a friend of mine. My brother casually mentioned that Leo reminded him of himself, not knowing that this child was actually my son, and very much a part of his family." Gradually unraveling the secrets took some time and continued to bring up painful feelings for Molly. "After my mother told my sister and brother, I felt bad all over again, but things gradually got better. My mother loves the visits now, which might be a little tense, but always good. I am sure that as Leo gets older, I will have more of a relationship with him."

Molly has since graduated from college and is living on the east coast. Leo is 8 years old now, and her experience of the open relationship has definitely changed:

Things aren't so raw anymore. In the first few years, I seemed to be lingering in a gray area, still figuring out my role. Now I feel very natural about the way our extended family works. I recently received a booklet of family pictures that Jeff and Allison had put together for Christmas. Looking through it, I didn't feel a twinge of regret, pain, or loss, because clearly there is none to be had. Leo and Zoe are literally glowing in all of the pictures, not only because they're vibrant individuals, but also in large part because Jeff and Allison have such

No one, at any point, ever mentioned to me the possibility that I could keep this child and how I might do that. It's not that I was ready to parent, but no one even gave me the right to consider that possibility.

— Molly, birth mother of Leo

enthusiasm for their kids, and encourage them to excel in whatever endeavor they choose.

Many of my friends are curious about how the relationship works. They're perplexed because when they come to my apartment they see Leo's and Zoe's artwork on my fridge, a picture of his whole family on the mantle, and I have cereal bowls that Leo made a few years ago that I often use. I'm sure it does seem strange to them that I have all these constant reminders, and I don't seem phased by them. Most people ask if it makes me sad, but these bits of memorabilia are part of my daily life—I don't really think about it too much. I just tell people that they're extended family—sort of like a favorite niece and nephew, but a bit closer.

I don't know how the future will unfold, but I know that I am committed to staying connected. I know that he is part of me, and since the birth father has disappeared, I feel even more strongly that Leo is my own creation. I watch him a lot when I visit him, and I enjoy observing his developing personality. I can see myself in him—my face in his face. He has so many personality quirks that my family totally recognizes: he is rambunctious, he is a little bit of a ham, and he's occasionally shy. He is like us and we are like a family.

In the first few years, I seemed to be lingering in a gray area, still figuring out my role. Now I feel very natural about the way our extended family works.

— Molly, birth mother of Leo

Evolving Openness

These families have continued to stay in close relationship over the last several years through phone calls, letters, e-mails, and photos sent via the Internet. The annual visits have evolved with the kids, who are now 8 and 12, visiting their birth families each summer on their own, being flown to and fro with a parent, a birth parent, or the birth grandmother. It's a big family event for each of the birth families when the children visit, and many relatives join in to be part of the ongoing welcoming committee. There is nothing in this arrangement that feels strange to the children—it is quite normal for them to be visiting these people who love them and welcome them as family. Of course for the adults, there are the logistics of arranging a smooth transition from one birth family's house to the other, and making arrangements that work for two very different birth families. But as Allison says, "We have only gotten closer as the years have gone by. We have had some sticky issues to resolve, but every time we take the risk to be honest and open, it has worked out." Allison and Jeff worked hard to lay a strong foundation for these relationships, and now they and their children have deeper and more meaningful ties with their extended birth families. (Allison, Jeff, Natalie, Abe, Molly and Jody: personal communication: 2003, 2004, & 2005)

CHAPTER 5

Becoming Extended Family

This chapter will explore openness through the lens of an extended family model, look at sibling relationships within the birth and adoptive family, and discuss the role openness plays in transracial adoption. Profiles will include an adoptive family that has developed strong ties with the birth grandmother; a family with transracially adopted children, who maintains a connection with a birth father; and a family that has extended open arms to its adoptive children's birth families across international borders.

The title of this chapter will be supportive to some, confusing to others, and overwhelming to a few. An adoptive parent might say "What? Extended family? I want to adopt a baby, I don't want to adopt another family." A birth mother might not be able to imagine contact with the adoptive family without experiencing emotional pain. The fact is that no matter what the type or frequency of contact, no matter how intimate or distant from each other they may become, birth and adoptive families will always be related to each other through their ties to the child. Shari Levine, the executive director of Open Adoption and Family Services in the Northwestern United States is adamant about this point:

> The birth family is a part of the adoptive family because they are the child's relatives. This will remain true regardless of the amount of contact they have. We would never accept the proposition that when we get married, we must cut off all ties to our family of origin to join our partner's family. Why would we ask that of our adopted children? (interview, 2004)

Patricia Martinez Dorner has been working in the field of adoption for over 25 years, and is the coauthor of *Children of Open Adoption.* (Silber & Dorner, 1989) She encourages us to look at birth and adoptive families in the same way we look at blended families:

We would never accept the proposition that when we get married, we must cut off all ties to our family of origin to join our partner's family. Why would we ask that of our adopted children?

— Shari Levine, director of Open Adoption and Family Services

Too often we consider adoptive family networks outside the realm of all other families. As a society, we have grown to understand and grapple with the unique dimensions and problems of blended families. We need to do the same for birth and adoptive families, who work on issues like every other family! If it is difficult to maintain contact, sometimes we need to pull away, sometimes we need to fight, sometimes we need to set better limits. When it isn't working, we need to use conflict resolution skills or seek help, just as other families might when they run into problems that they cannot solve (interview, 2004).

Many of the adoptive parents interviewed here spoke about wanting more openness after the first year, but found that the birth parents needed to create some distance before they could reconnect when the child was older.

An extended birth family may include the birth parents, birth grandparents, uncles, aunts, brothers and sisters, and other children of the birth parents. In order to invite them in, we need to consider some of the obstacles that birth family members face. Many birth parents, and often their own parents, have come to believe the prevailing messages about adoption. They may be under the impression that if they don't have contact, they will be able to put the grief and suffering of the adoption process behind them. The birth grandparents may be afraid of openness because they are concerned that their child will be hurt once again if the adoptive family discontinues contact. For some birth family members, the pregnancy may have been a shameful experience, and they are afraid that ongoing contact will deepen their embarrassment.

When birth parents are too young or emotionally immature to sustain a healthy relationship, or if they are having a difficult time with the grieving process, other members of the birth family can maintain the connection. Occasionally mental health issues or substance abuse keeps birth parents from being able to have a healthy relationship with the adoptive family. In these cases, the adoptive parents might put limits on contact and choose to stay in touch with a healthier member of the birth family. Helping extended birth family members become involved will require an understanding of the obstacles they face, and educating them about the positive role they can play in the life of the child. Often an experienced open adoption professional can assist with this task, which requires cultural sensitivity and respect for the unique challenges a birth family is facing.

After the first year or more of seeing the baby develop and thrive in the adoptive family, some birth parents may separate themselves in order to go about rebuilding their lives. Many of the adoptive parents interviewed here spoke about wanting *more* openness after the first year, but found that the birth parents needed to create some distance before they could reconnect when the child was older. When that happens, the birth grandparents may become the major link between the families.

There are few models in popular culture for birth parent involvement with adoptive families, and there are even fewer for the extended birth family, so it is natural that awkwardness affects the beginning of these relationships. Imagine being an actor in a play but no one has given you the script! The extended adoptive family might have some reluctance to meet the birth family because they are unsure about their right to claim the child if the birth family is still in the picture. An adoptive grandparent might be thinking, 'If she is the *real* birth grandmother, what does that make me?' These feelings may lead to competition, but when adoptive family members claim this child as their own, they are less likely to feel competitive. Shirley, an adoptive grandparent confessed: "I was a little jealous at first, and wondered if the birth grandmother would feel she was more important to the child than me. But as I grew more comfortable with my role, I stopped worrying about her, and focused on my grandson."

Sometimes birth parents may worry that their family's involvement might affect their own relationship with the adoptive family. Brenda Romanchik, a birth parent and an advocate for openness in adoption, tells us about her struggle when her parents were developing their own relationship with her birth son and his adoptive family:

> I was afraid that my parents would jeopardize *my* relationship with the adoptive parents by being too doting, so I tried to curb their behavior by telling them what I thought was acceptable. The adoptive mom laid my fears to rest, told me not to worry, and said that she could handle my parents. As I became less concerned about my parents doing something wrong to mess things up for *me*, I was able to see all of the things they were doing right for *him* (interview, 2005).

Sometimes simple and direct communication is all that is needed to find out what is OK and what is not. A birth grandmother named Gloria recalls, "I wanted to make quilts and send special gifts, but I wasn't sure if I would be stepping over a line. So I got up the courage to ask the adoptive parents, and they said yes, of course. It meant so much to me to be able to let him know that he is loved by this side of his family too."

Another issue that might arise is that the age of the birth grandparents is frequently closer to that of the adoptive parents, and they may share similar values or lifestyles. This could lead to the adoptive parents forging closer ties with them than the birth parents. Haley, a 21-year-old birth mother, was distressed when she discovered that the adoptive parents and her own mother had been discussing how she was handling her emotions. This made her feel as though she was still the child, and the adults were talking about her. When she asked the adoptive parents not to divulge any information without her consent, she was able to claim her role as an adult partner in the arrangement. Being so young, and having had many of the decisions about the adoption made by her parents, it was especially important that

Haley was able to carve out a relationship with the adoptive parents that was not controlled by her mother.

At the same time that adoptive parents need to respect the primacy of the relationship with the birth parents, it is important to recognize that open adoption is about birth *families*, not just birth parents. Brenda Romanchik agrees:

> I have seen situations where birth mothers do not want the child to have contact with the birth father or other birth family members. She might have good reasons for not wanting other birth family members to be involved, but the focus needs to be on the child's needs, not solely about the needs of the birth mother. If a birth mother has been unable to stay in contact, and the adoptive family knows that there are other birth family members who might add to a child's life, they have a right to pursue them (interview, 2005).

When members of the birth family are not in agreement with the adoption plan, or they have not been involved in the selection of the adoptive family, they may feel resentful of their status. These family members may choose to stay away from the adoptive family, but sometimes they participate without having resolved their feelings. Mary McNalley, the mother of four children through open adoption, found this to be particularly challenging. "Adoption was chosen by the birth mother, and we were selected by her, but other members of the birth family did not feel it was the right choice. These members felt such grief and anger, it sometimes felt like they were going overboard in pushing the openness just to see if they could get a rise out of us." Staying the course eventually provided benefits to everyone, and Mary was relieved when these same people allowed a relationship to blossom that included healthier boundaries. This might have been an ideal time for a counseling or mediation session to identify and cope with the birth family members' reactions to the adoption.

If a birth mother has been unable to stay in contact, and the adoptive family knows that there are other birth family members who might add to a child's life, they have a right to pursue them.

— Brenda Romanchik, adoption educator and advocate

Unexpected Extended Family

Rob and Rhonda are the parents of Hannah, their biological child, and Isaac, who was adopted at birth. It was only after they decided to take some risks that they evolved into becoming an extended family with their son's birth mother and his birth grandmother (interview, 2005). As you read their story, keep these questions in mind: What allowed Rob and Rhonda to be receptive to openness? The two families live relatively close to each other: What issues might arise between adoptive families and birth parents who live close to each other? What helped lay the foundation for openness in this family?

From left to right: Rhonda, Debbie, Isaac and Hannah. Back row: Rob. Rob and Rhonda are the adoptive parents of Isaac. Hannah is their biological daughter. Debbie is the birth grandmother of Isaac.

Rob, Father of Hannah and Isaac

If you had told me 8 years ago that my daughter Hannah would be staying overnight at my son's birth grandmother's house, I would have run away as fast as I could! We had some of the same ideas about openness that most people have: annual visits and photos a few times a year. We never intended our relationship with the birth mother and her family to become this close. What helped me was that I had a stepfather who was totally my Dad, so I had a pretty inclusive model of what makes a family.

We could have chosen the minimal amount of contact with the birth family, but we decided to open ourselves up, even when we were scared. Before the birth, we were invited over to the birth grandmother's home for our first meeting with the extended birth family that included brothers, sisters, aunts, and uncles. You've got to understand that this is not something that I would normally do: enter a home of total strangers who might be looking at me to see if I am the right guy to father one of their own. But I did it and looking back, I can see why they needed to have that meeting.

We don't know what kind of contact Isaac will want to have with his birth mother when he is 10 or 15, but we do know that we didn't want to live in fear of contact with a birth family member. If we only saw

Becoming Extended Family

a birth family once a year, we think *that* would be awkward. It's not uncomfortable because we see them all the time and our kids totally get it! Isaac and Hannah have absolutely no problem with having three sets of grandparents. Adults make this all so much more complicated than it needs to be. To the kids, this is just another person that loves them and that they love back.

The best advice I would give to adoptive and birth parents is to remember why you are doing this. It's not just a matter of making sure you are comfortable. Insecurities will come up, but it is important to see if you can stretch outside of your comfort zone for the benefit of the child. You have to try to remember that this isn't all about us.

Rhonda, an Adoptee, Biological Mother of
Hannah and Adoptive Mother of Isaac

When I was first exposed to open adoption I was shocked! All the information I had about where I had come from was barely enough to fit into a little envelope, so it was hard for me to understand the need for openness. I didn't think it was such a big deal to have a connection with one's genetic family until I had my own daughter. She was the first person in my entire life who was related to me, and seeing someone who looked like me was absolutely amazing.

Part of what has allowed me to be open to our son's birth parents, is that I knew how I would feel if my own daughter placed a child for adoption. If I were a grandparent, how would I feel about never seeing that child or not having any role in his life? My son Isaac's birth grandmother Debbie, teaches my daughter Hannah crocheting, does art projects, and occasionally takes her for an overnight stay. Who wouldn't want their kids to have more of this kind of love?

Don't get me wrong—there were awkward times in the beginning. When Isaac was about a month old, his birth mother Emily asked if she could have a little "alone time" with him. I thought "What exactly does *alone time* mean?" I felt like I had done all this open stuff and still she wanted more. Then I read some of the materials on open adoption that helped me remember that this is not just about Emily having a relationship with *us,* but it is about her having a relationship with Isaac.

A few months later, Emily asked if we could bring Isaac to her workplace so she could show him to her work mates. At first this also seemed awkward, but then I realized that she wanted them to see that she really did have a baby, and that he was in good hands. When

I could look at it from her perspective, I could understand that this would help her with a sense of closure. At the same time that I felt empathy for her situation, I also respected my own needs and boundaries. I was tempted to invite Emily and Debbie to come with me for Isaac's first haircut, but then I realized I wanted that for myself. When we took him to the first day of kindergarten, I am glad that it was just his Dad and I, but my heart was so filled with love that I talked to Debbie and Emily later that night about his first day in school.

As an adoptee, I am definitely curious about finding my birth family, but I would never do anything to hurt my parents. They say that they understand, but they always get a little teary about it, so I don't feel fully free to search. I never want Isaac to have to feel that way. He will have no unanswered questions like the ones I have had all of my life. Openness will allow him to not create pie-in-the-sky fantasies about his birth family, or the other extreme of imagining all the worse things they could be. I want people to understand that open adoption is a gift not a burden. Some friends have said to me, "Don't worry, in a few years, she will move on and you won't have her in your life so much." On the contrary, we hope we will have a relationship with the birth family forever and we want that for our son.

Debbie, Birth Grandmother

The only expectation that I had about open adoption was that my daughter Emily would share pictures and information with me. After the birth, my daughter asked me to take the baby from her because she was feeling weak. I took my first-born grandchild from my only daughter's arms and placed him in the arms of his adoptive mother. I don't think Abraham could have felt any worse when he placed *his* Isaac on the altar, because I felt like I was giving away my own flesh and blood. I never dreamt that the future might hold a relationship for myself and my husband with our birth grandchild, but after the birth, Rob and Rhonda invited us to their home, and I knew this relationship would be different.

As our relationship evolved, Rhonda told me that she, Rob, and her extended family had discussed it, and they wanted to call us Grandma and Grandpa. My husband couldn't believe it and e-mailed Rob saying, "You better be sure of this, because once you say yes, we will want to have grandparent spoiling rights!" Rob wrote back in the largest font possible: "LET THE SPOILING BEGIN."

> *I want people to understand that open adoption is a gift—not a burden. Some friends have said to me, "Don't worry, in a few years, she will move on and you won't have her in your life so much." On the contrary, we hope we will have a relationship with the birth family forever and we want that for our son.*
>
> — Rhonda, adoptive mother of Isaac

Before the birth when Rob and Rhonda visited our home, I had all of our family photo albums out so that they could see Isaac's genealogy. That simple gesture made it clear that I was there to answer any and all questions about our family, and that helped build the ties we have today. The biggest surprise in all of this is that we have grown incredibly close with Hannah, their oldest daughter, who is 13. I go to a lot of her and Isaac's soccer games, school plays, and they each stay overnight sometimes. My advice to birth families and adoptive families would be to share who you are in the deepest way possible, because that will help build the relationship.

Sibling Relationships

Birth parents may have had one or more children before or after placement of one of their children for adoption. Thus, children in adoptive families may have full or half biological siblings living either with a birth parent, another birth relative, in another adoptive family, or in the foster system. In either case, their relationships run the gamut of very close, to very distant, to no contact at all. Melina and Roszia, the authors of *The Open Adoption Experience* (1993) remind us about the differences between siblings raised together and ones raised apart:

> Siblings are children who share the experience of growing up together. There is a closeness that comes from being the only people who know what it is like to grow up in their families. This sense of shared memories and experience often keeps siblings close long into adulthood. For this reason, children who grow up together in an adoptive family feel like brother and sisters, even if they are not genetically related. (page 288)

Sibling relationships with brothers and sisters who live outside of the adoptive family may be special, but even when they are in regular contact, they are usually not as close as siblings who are raised together.

The fact that there are siblings may help the birth and adoptive families develop a deeper understanding of the need for connection, but it also adds additional issues that need to be addressed. What should we call the other child? Half brother? Birth brother? Jody is the birth mother of Zoe, whose adoptive family paid a visit after Jody gave birth to her second child. "I noticed that Zoe didn't want to be called the baby's sister, as though it would not be respectful to her relationship with her own family." Allison, Zoe's adoptive mother, knew that she didn't want to get hung up on what the siblings should call each other, and decided that they would refer to the baby by its name instead of the sibling relationship. What to call a sibling may depend on the type of relationship, the geographical closeness, the frequency of visits, the age of the children, and how the parents feel about

Making Room in Our Hearts

it. Danny, profiled in chapter 2, is a young adult and has had an ongoing relationship with his siblings in his birth mother's family. Neither he nor his sisters consider themselves "half," as their relationship has evolved over the years even though they did not grow up together.

Several adoptive parents reported that when they communicated to their child about the birth parents having other children in a matter-of-fact way, that the children seemed to take it in their stride. One reported that her adopted daughter was glad to see that her birth mother was having other children. Mary McNalley recalls, "Our 9-year-old daughter's birth mother recently married and has a baby of her own. She is savoring all the firsts with her son, and we have talked about her realization of all she missed with her first baby, our daughter. That has been painful for her and for us at times, but our daughter said she was so happy that her birth mom was finally getting the opportunity to be a mom."

One adoptive mother, Harriet, remarked, "The future is a long time and who knows what will happen in these relationships between siblings down the road?" Like many adoptive parents, Harriet, age 53, is an older parent who thinks ahead to the day when she might not be around, but hopes that her child's relationships with her siblings will deepen in later years. Her 12-year-old daughter has begun to have weeklong annual visits with her 9-year-old brother who lives with the birth mother. "I keep the door open, and my daughter and her birth sibling can do what they want with that as they mature, but at least I am giving them the opportunity to know each other enough to make that choice."

It is important to remember that the adoptee's siblings that remain in the birth family or were adopted into a different family, are related and would have grown up with each other if it weren't for difficult circumstances. Many siblings that were separated from each other in early childhood have spent their lives looking for their missing brother or sister. Staying in touch and keeping the doors open to other siblings is a vital role that adoptive and birth parents can play.

Openness and Transracial Adoption

Maintaining connections with the birth family in a transracial adoption may offer some important benefits. Most often, a child of color is placed with a European-American (white) family where the physical differences often make it an obvious adoption. Openness allows for not only a connection to a birth family member, but also to the adoptee's racial and cultural heritage. Gail Steinberg and Beth Hall, the authors of *Inside Transracial Adoption* (2000), have been educating the adoption community about issues in transracial adoption through their organization Pact, An Adoption Alliance:

I keep the door open, and my daughter and her birth sibling can do what they want with that as they mature, but at least I am giving them the opportunity to know each other enough to make that choice.

— Harriet, an adoptive mother

In transracial adoption, the importance of building relationships is intensified because the birth family represents the child's race. If children do not feel positive about their birth family, they may have difficulty integrating their birth cultures. They may think that people of their race or ethnicity rejected them, because people of a different race adopted them. When children are supported in maintaining positive relationships with birth family members, they are more likely to feel positive about their heritage and themselves. (page 140)

Recently, my daughter was talking to a new friend several feet in front of me, and the other child asked my daughter, "Is that your Mom?" My daughter immediately answered, "Yes, that's my Mom. I'm adopted—that's why we look different." My daughter seemed especially attuned to the fact that the girl might have been wondering how a woman who looked different from her could be her mother. The girl might merely have been wondering if I was her mom, and not even have thought about how we looked different. My daughter assumed that her friend had noticed the physical difference, as she is so aware of it, especially as she enters her teen years. We have tried to incorporate our daughter's birth culture into our family life, and one of the most important steps was forming a relationship with Carlos, who is a link to her birth family. No matter how many Mexican-American holidays or festivities we go to, no matter how diverse our school district is, having ties to a person of my daughter's ethnic heritage who loves her, is priceless. It is important that adoptive parents create ways to include other people of their child's ethnicity and race in their lives on a regular basis, in addition to birth family members.

Another area that is of vital importance in transracial adoption is teaching children how to deal with racism in all of its insidious and most obvious forms. Children of color will undoubtedly experience a range of attitudes and behaviors that are implicitly or explicitly racist. From being looked at as someone who might not be as bright in math, to being more closely followed in stores as teenagers, children of color will require support, teaching, and encouragement as they develop ways to identify and cope with racism. Organizations such as Pact can be of immense help to adoptive parents as they try to teach their children how to deal with racism, and birth family members can also offer insights about how they cope with, and resist the effects of racism. However, it is important to not solely rely on a birth family member to teach a child about racism.

Staying in Touch with a Birth Father in a Transracial Adoption

In the next profile, Katie and Matt speak honestly about the bond they have formed with the birth mother of their daughter Lily, and with Johnny

Bottom, left to right: Reed and Lily. Top: left to right: Katie, Parker, Johnny, and Matt. Katie and Matt are the adoptive parents of Reed and Lily and Parker is their biological son. Johnny is the birth father of Reed.

the birth father to Reed. Both are transracially adopted children. As you read this profile, keep in mind the following questions: what thoughts and feelings do you have about a child being raised in a family of another race or ethnic background? What are some of the challenges that a child will face growing up in a family of another race or ethnicity (Interview, 2005)?

Mathew, Adoptive Father of Lily and Reed

Our 12-year-old biological son has severe physical disabilities, so as a family, we were *already* stared at in the grocery store. My wife and I had many complex feelings about transracial adoption because it raised the question of how much more "different" we were willing to look as a family. We grappled with these questions alone, as our agency rarely talked about the issues involved in raising kids of color. We finally arrived at our decision because of the diverse community where we live that would allow our children to grow up knowing people of many different races.

We thought that by choosing open adoptions, our children would be less likely to be plagued by issues of abandonment and rejection, and that the birth families would not wonder if a child they passed on the street could be their own. It seemed like the best way to provide for better mental health, and fewer lifelong struggles for our children. Even if it did cause us some additional hassles, we thought the benefits to our children would outweigh any disturbance to us.

We thought that by choosing open adoptions, our children would be less likely to be plagued by issues of abandonment and rejection, and that the birth families would not wonder if a child they passed on the street could be their own.

— Mathew, adoptive father of Lily and Reed

When we met our daughter Lily's birth mother for the first time, her own mother was with her. The birth grandmother had placed a child for adoption when she was very young, and had wondered about that child her whole life, which definitely influenced her daughter to continue contact with us. The birth mother knew that seeing the baby was going to hurt, so she limited contact in the first year, but we now have about two to three visits a year. She went through a period where she had difficulty making good decisions, but we decided that we were never going to lecture her about her having other children. We accept who she is, and have decided that we were not going to place ourselves in the role as rescuer, which has helped all of us handle this relationship.

Lily's birth mother is happily married now, and has two other children, so her life is more stable. Lily was the flower girl in her wedding and I know that was a special and treasured experience for them both. When we visit the birth mother, we see her mom, her sister, her niece, her husband, and her kids. I have put these relationships in the context of distant relatives: you carry them in your lives, but you don't always see them regularly.

Katie, Adoptive Mother of Lily and Reed

It took me a while to embrace transracial adoption. I had to do my own grieving over having had a child with serious special needs, and then not being able to have more children after that. At first, I thought that I didn't want to stand out any more, because I already stood out with an obviously disabled child. But as time went on, I realized that I cared more about becoming a mom than what my kids looked like. I have come to think of standing out as a teaching opportunity.

The relationship between our family and Reed's birth father Johnny has developed steadily over the past 8 years. We first met him before Reed was born, and it took a lot of guts for a young black man in braids and tattoos to come to a meeting with our lawyer. We learned that Johnny had a drug history, so we wanted to take it slow until we built up trust in the relationship. He has always been very honest with us, and as long as Johnny was OK at our house, he was welcome. Once he came by and my parents were here. My Dad doesn't exactly have a history of hanging out with young African-American men, but he was watching a game and Johnny just dropped down on the couch and they talked football.

We are fortunate to live in a well-integrated neighborhood where Reed has many examples of strong black males. These friends and neighbors are influential because they are good husbands, fathers, and citizens, and Reed sees them regularly. Johnny is not the only black

Our son knows that he is part of our family, not out of abandonment or indifference, but out of his birth father's love.

— Katie, adoptive mother of Reed

Left to right: Johnny and Reed. Johnny is Reed's birth father.

male that he can identify with, but their relationship will always be an important influence as Reed grows older and his understanding of adoption evolves. We have had many candid conversations with Johnny about discrimination, and many of the racial issues Reed will face as he matures. Our son knows that he is part of our family, not out of abandonment or indifference, but out of his birth father's love.

When Johnny is away, he calls to touch base: it is like *we* have become a home base for *him*. All of my kids have grown to love him, and he has instinctively known to bring presents for all of them, not just for Reed. Assumptions and judgments can get in the way of seeing people's humanity. Johnny loves Reed and wants the best for him and that love transcends our differences.

Johnny: Birth Father of Reed

In the beginning, I wasn't cool with this situation at all. Black men catch a lot of it for not taking care of their own kids. It was never my intention to give away my son, but his birth mother just didn't think she could hang with it. I know I will never have the relationship with my son that I wanted, but when Reed grows up, he will understand that I wanted to be a part of his life. I visited him for the first time about a month after he was born, and I had a really hard time with it. I left their house and drove around in my car crying, that's how hard it hurt. I would visit once or twice a month and every time I left, it hurt real bad. But I finally could see that Matt and Katie were bending over backwards to make it possible for me to have a relationship with Reed. They really meant that I was welcome in their home, and I could feel that.

I want to be there for Reed to tell him that it is OK for him to be a nerd if that is what it takes to learn. Because it's the nerds that get the "Beemers." I am just making myself available because he may be mixed race, but America is going to see him and treat him as a black man. That's what I can help him with because this is a real racist world. If you saw me—I got tattoos, I look ghetto, but Matt and Katie have always judged me by how I act. They know I have a good heart. I had never been close to any white folks in my whole life, and now they are raising my son. We look at life through different eyes, but they understand me. I know people who look at me like I was stupid for doing this. They say, "Why would you go and let white people raise your kid?" I've gotten into arguments about this, but I tell them that it is about Reed and what is best for him.

My family and parents still haven't accepted the situation. They look at his picture and they can see how much he looks like me. It is not accepted in my community, and they are still upset that he isn't being raised by my family. They also don't understand this open adoption thing. They ask me why I don't bring Reed to visit them, when they live four hours away from where Matt and Katie live. I tell them that you have got to build some trust first before a big visit like that. When I get a picture of Reed, it's worth more than a million dollars to me. I was very closed-minded coming into this situation, but Matt and Katie have let me build a bond with my child. They are the best people I know, and I'm cool with the situation now. I heard his first words. I saw him take some of his first steps. This open adoption thing can really work. I couldn't ask for anything greater.

Creating Extended Family across Borders

Many adoptive families have turned to their children's countries of origin for cultural and ethnic ties, and some have taken the pioneering steps toward openness between themselves and their children's birth family. Leceta Chisholm Guibault is a Canadian woman, who with her husband Jean has two children through international adoption: 15-year-old daughter Kahleah is from Guatemala, and 12-year-old Tristan is from Colombia. The degree of openness this family has established with Kahleah's foster parent family and Tristan's extended birth family is not typical. Even today,

Tristan and his biological sister Katherine, who he met for the first time when he was 10 years old.

the quality of openness they have established would be viewed as virtually impossible in most international adoptions. The fact that they have transformed what is usually an extremely closed system into one that is open can serve as a window into the possibilities for the future.

Leceta remembers:

From the day our children were placed in our arms, we knew that one day we would travel as a family to the lands of their birth. I did not want my children to grow up as adult adoptees who had never been back to where they were born. By then, they might be scared to go back, or no one would have any memory of them. We have supported our daughter in maintaining contact with her foster family in Guatemala, and it has provided her with an important link to her past. When I asked her what she liked about it, she said at age 9, "It feels good to be remembered." We knew we would try to do the same with our son Tristan's birth family, who lived in Colombia (interview, 2006).

After Tristan's birth, Leceta and Jean were relieved to receive the social history report from which they learned the name and age of his birth mother, along with names of siblings, birth father, and maternal grandparents:

I also received copies of an interview with the birth mother where she explained her story of "why." My heart broke for her. Her love for my/our son was obvious. Her final recorded words were, "I love my son. I do not want him to suffer with me." It occurred to me that in order to give her child a better life she was being sentenced to a life of grief and guilt, not knowing if she had made the right decision; not knowing if her child was dead or alive. Her crime? Inescapable poverty. I noticed that the social history report included a complete address for her and I knew I was going to contact her some day.

For the past 10 years they have been in contact with most members of both Tristan's maternal and paternal birth families. "We have sent them videos and hundreds of family photos. Tristan has a complete album of birth family photos of his birth mother, siblings, grandparents, aunts, uncles, cousins, and a scrapbook full of letters. My son knows where he came from, knows who he looks like, and knows why he was adopted." There are cultural, language, and vast economic differences between Tristan's two families, but they also share some similarities. "We share a religious faith, a strong work ethic, and a commitment to education and to our families. Most importantly, we share love for the same little boy."

After eight years of communicating by mail, phone, and e-mail, they decided to travel to Colombia to meet the birth families in person. Knowing that, "mixed in with the joy and excitement of reunion there will be some grief, sadness, and even confusion," they made their plans. Anticipating the special trip, Tristan was 10 years old when he wrote for *Adoptive Families* magazine, "I am going with my family to Colombia where I will see my brother, sisters, and birth mother, and I will hug them and kiss them. I never got to say good-bye to them because I could not talk. This is a trip that I have always wanted and will never forget."

Shortly after the journey Tristan recalled in an article for *Adoptive Families*:

I was so excited to see her that my heart almost stopped. When they arrived we all looked at each other and the adults cried because adults are adults. I was just happy. My birth family looked just like their pictures. It felt like I knew them all my life. I was really looking forward to seeing my brother because I already had a sister, but no brothers. He looks like me. He runs fast like me. He climbs trees like me. He likes to swim like me. He did not speak English and I did not speak Spanish, but it did not matter. My birth mother Piedad cried when she saw me. My Mommy Leceta cried too. I think they cried

I was so excited to see my birth mother that my heart almost stopped. My birth family looked just like their pictures. It felt like I knew them all my life.

— Tristan, a 10-year-old adoptee from Colombia

because they were happy. Maybe they were sad a little too. I think they were sad because we live so far away. When I saw my birth mother I felt really happy because I thought about her for years and now I know that she thought about me too.

This child's experience tells us so vividly what it is like to claim one's birth family and country, even if they are thousands of miles away. Both the adoptive and birth families put years of preparation and heartfelt consideration into making this reunion the best it could be for everyone involved, including the siblings in both families. As Leceta comments:

It took a lot of understanding on our part to make this work, but once we extended the invitation, the doors opened widely. I have received negative feedback from some adoptive parents who have said, "They are *his* family—not yours. He should have been able to decide as an adult." They did not have the opportunity to develop this kind of relationship, but this is *normal* for our family: we have extended family in Colombia just like we have extended family in England. When we visit Colombia, we can see Tristan's face in his birth family, and we can see a genetic resemblance in the larger community. You can tell that he is so proud to see who he looks like (interview, 2005).

The sense of well being that openness seems to have brought these children is surpassed only by the joy these newfound relationships have brought to Tristan's birth mother, Piedad, who also wrote for *Adoptive Families* magazine:

Being the mother that I am, I never thought to give my son up for adoption. I don't have words to express my feelings of how I felt— finding myself so young and alone with two very young children and to have to leave another one to be adopted. I asked myself many times what would be the life of my child. My maternal instinct told me that he was well; but the conscience accuses you and betrays you, causing you to think the worse. I was also disturbed by thoughts that maybe he was not adopted and still at the orphanage and never found a family, or brothers or sisters or parents to love him. I also worried that he would hate me and have a thousand questions about why I had to give him away. I worried about how I would answer those questions.

My hopes were that in that time my child would be adopted by a good family that would give him a good education, to understand when he did a mischief and did not mistreat him. I hoped they would give him medicine when was sick and a lot of love. I thought of him and I cried for him during the two long years until I received the first letter from his parents, and learned he did not suffer. Through the letters, pictures, and videos, I learned that not everything is bad about adoption.

With the adoptive family of my son, I describe a marvelous relationship! Open adoption has been something very positive for me because the contact can fulfill what mothers seek—to know their child is alive. My son can now better understand the fact that he does have two families and he is something of mine, but that he doesn't belong to me. Today I feel very well, since I know that my son is with people that have truly accepted my child as their own and they give all the love that parents can give their children. They are excellent people and my son will always be in good hands and he will be the same as born to them. Adoption is a good option. Adoption is a better choice than abandonment or abortion. I want my boy to know that I love him and always wanted what was best for him and that is why I chose adoption and not to kill him in my womb or to throw him away. To me this is the decision of a good mother. I am here if and when he needs me.

Hundred of thousands of women around the world have relinquished children for adoption and are faced with shame, stigma, secrecy, guilt, and years of grief—most without resources to help them deal with these feelings. But the experience of openness in international adoption can bring some of the same relief that it does in domestic adoption. Leceta continues:

I have seen benefits for everyone with this degree of openness. His siblings in Colombia don't live with the shadow of a child that was relinquished. They know him, see his pictures, and hear his voice. Piedad has said many times that this has made her a better mother because she is not wondering and worrying about Tristan and no longer feels shame or regret about her decision.

Some of the material in Tristan and Piedad's profiles appeared in *Adoptive Families* magazine and we gratefully acknowledge permission to reprint it here.

Some of the material in Tristan and Piedad's profile appeared in *Adoptive Families* magazine, and we gratefully acknowledge permission to print it here.

> *Open adoption has been something very positive for me. My son can now better understand the fact that he does have two families and he is something of mine, but that he doesn't belong to me.*
>
> — Piedad, Colombian birth mother of Tristan

CHAPTER 6

Openness in the Public Adoption System

The understanding that maintaining family ties is important for the adopted person's sense of self is increasingly influencing the practices of the public foster-adoption system. The adoption of children via the public child welfare system is very different from the adoption of newborns via agencies or attorneys. This chapter will examine some of those differences, and take a look at openness in the public system through the lens of several innovative programs. Finally, two families, each with three children adopted through the foster-adoption programs, describe the ways they have addressed the unique challenges of maintaining family ties with birth families.

Keeping Family Ties in the Public System

One of the differences between independent or private adoption and the foster-adoption system is that birth parents *choose* adoption in the private sector, although difficult social and emotional circumstances often force their decision. Most birth parents in the public system do not volunteer to relinquish their children, but find themselves unable to overcome the effects of chemical dependency or mental illness that frequently go hand-in-hand with the effects of poverty. In the child welfare system, children have been taken out of their families, and placed in foster homes because of abuse, neglect, or the inability of parents to adequately provide for their children. Some of these children are removed from their families at birth, but most are removed between the ages of 2 and 6 and are placed in a foster family, or a series of foster families, to await rulings by the courts. After a process that may take several years, they are either returned to their birth families who have participated in a reunification process, or placed for adoption.

Historically, when the termination of parental rights was completed, unless the child was placed with extended family, little or no contact occurred between the adoptive family and the birth parents. However, since the early 1990s, there has been increased understanding of the importance of helping the child maintain continuity, and avoid total separation from his or her birth family. There has been a growth of many innovative programs whose purpose is to make the adoption process less adversarial, and increase the possibilities for children to maintain safe ties to their birth families. We will look at openness through the lens of these programs, because several public agencies declined to speak on the record.

Cheryl Roberts is the social work supervisor for Lilliput, a nonprofit adoption agency in California that has been one of the forerunners in promoting openness in the public system:

> We make it clear that it is not in the best interest of children to be cut off from all that they have known, and having an abrupt end to familial relationships is almost always traumatic for children. It is difficult for adoptive parents to empathize with birth parents who may have caused harm to their children, but we help them understand that it is in their interest, as well as their child's, to find something positive about the birth parents. Some birth parents are not healthy enough for visits, so the adoptive family might need to have limited contact. Other children have been so traumatized by abuse that it isn't appropriate to consider visits, but we keep talking about the connection (interview, 2003).

Carolyn Mitchell, a clinical social worker with over 20 years in child welfare, agrees. "Good boundaries are vital in protecting the child, the adoptive parents, and the birth parents, who also suffer when they behave in inappropriate ways with their children." Carolyn has been a trainer for the Kinship Center, one of the early pioneers in promoting openness. "Many of the birth parents had to relinquish their children because of the effects of drug use, so there has to be agreement that no contact will take place unless all parties are clean and sober. Visits might be supervised or contact could just be calls or letters, but we need to remember that birth parents can and do change."

Birth parents are sometimes able to make changes in their lives precisely because they are not facing the burden of parenting. Others may feel an obligation to stay clean and sober so they can continue to maintain contact with their children. Susan is a 23-year-old birth mother whose story illustrates how openness in adoption has served as a motivating force in her life. As a child, Susan had been physically and emotionally abused by her mother and taken out of the home by Child Protective Services on several occasions, but always returned to face additional years of abuse. It is no wonder that as an adult, she found herself unable to protect herself in an emotionally and physically abusive relationship with a partner. She voluntarily relinquished

It is not in the best interest of children to be cut off from all that they have known, and having an abrupt end to familial relationships is almost always traumatic for children.

— Cheryl Roberts, Lilliput Adoptions

her two children at ages 2 and 4, through her county's adoption program, because she recognized that she was not emotionally or financially able to support them.

The adoptive parents of her two children decided they could support a certain degree of openness, especially since Susan had never intentionally hurt her children, and had voluntarily relinquished them. They agreed to letters and pictures and an annual visit, and Susan has been adamant that those visits helped her stay alive, "If it weren't for those kids, I would have been out of here by now. But it really matters to me. I want them to feel good about themselves, so I keep it together and always show up in a good state. Knowing that they are in a good home, and that I can visit them is what makes my life worthwhile."

Involuntary relinquishment of one's rights to parent often leaves birth parents feeling ashamed that they have "lost" their children, and they want to distance themselves from the adoptive family and everything that reminds them of that experience. Carolyn Mitchell encourages adoption professionals to create programs that acknowledge the damage done by involuntary relinquishments.

> We do this by encouraging birth parents to have an active role in the decision-making process. We want these birth parents to feel better about themselves and their decision to assist with permanency planning for their child. Our whole society should have a stake in the long-term emotional health of birth parents that have had to relinquish their children. When we don't support them adequately with programs that include counseling and education, we increase the likelihood that there will be more unplanned pregnancies, more drug abuse, and other forms of self-destructive behavior (interview, 2003).

Supporting Openness in the Public Sector

The Consortium for Children is a non-profit organization based in northern California that specializes in permanency planning mediation, a model of intervention that is slowly making important changes in the child welfare system. Mediation is offered *before* the termination of parental rights, so that birth parents and potential adoptive parents have the opportunity to come to mutual agreements that will be good for the child. This is always a voluntary process that either party can stop at any time, and is done with the assistance of a specially trained adoption mediator. It involves a series of meetings that might include birth parents, adoptive parents, social workers, foster parents, and others who have been part of a child's life and have a stake in his or her future. Tom Rutherford, the former Clinical Director of the Consortium for Children, reminds us that:

Our whole society should have a stake in the long-term emotional health of birth parents that have had to relinquish their children. When we don't support them, we increase the likelihood that there will be more unplanned pregnancies, more drug abuse, and other forms of self-destructive behavior."

— Carolyn Mitchell, a social worker

Preadoptive parents usually reject openness because it does *not* meet their fantasies: they come to adoption wanting a child, not an extended family. Birth parents embrace contact, because it *does* meet their fantasies. They hope that if they enter into a relationship and if it goes well, they will not lose all contact with their child. In mediation, we ask both parties to consider the best interest of the child. Once we assure adoptive families that their address, their personal life, and even their full identities can remain confidential, they are often more than willing to enter into these relationships (interview, 2003).

Written agreements arising out of the mediation process may include the type and frequency of contact, who will initiate the contact, and under what circumstances the agreements would be voided. Concerns for safety and confidentiality of the adoptive parents might be addressed by having supervised visits in the birth grandmother's home, or with someone designated by the court. Concerns about drug use may be addressed by requiring that the birth parents participate in treatment before contact visits will be discussed. As in all other types of adoption arrangements, openness in the public system is a continuum and may start with letters and lead to more contact only as both parties develop trust and are able to honor appropriate boundaries.

Susan Quash-Mah is the manager of Teamwork for Children in Oregon, which was the first program in the country to offer permanency planning mediation. Susan feels strongly about the importance of assuring adoptive parents about the continuum of openness:

> We never encourage adoptive parents to stretch beyond their realm of comfort, so the mediated agreements seek to establish the *minimal* contact that will provide some continuity to the child. Birth parents will never be penalized for not showing up, but if they attempt to exceed the agreed upon limits, they may lose their rights for visits. If a birth or adoptive parent reneges on their agreements, either party can go back to the court to have the agreements mediated again, but the adoption itself is never in question (interview, 2003).

All around the country, judges, attorneys, and social workers are looking more closely at public adoption practices and their effects on the children they are serving. Many agree that social workers in the public system need to be more thoroughly educated about the benefits of openness to the child, the adoptive family, and the birth parents. Susan Quash-Mah agrees:

> We need to change the system in many ways, and one of the ways is to stop looking at the end of the legal adoption process as "finalization." The child may have a permanent home, but our job is not over. We talk about "child-centered" adoption, but we need to change our

allocation of resources to support these families over time, because it is in our society's best interest to support these ongoing connections. These children were born to parents who left genetic, cultural, psychological, and spiritual marks that cannot be altered by adoption. You can alter the child's legal status, but these are ties that go above the law. These children were born into the world connected, and we need to support their entry into the new homes, by acknowledging that first attachment.

When adoptions take place through the foster-adoption system there are often siblings involved, and their presence presents unique challenges. Either older siblings have already been removed from the home and may be in foster placement or adopted, or younger siblings are still with the birth family, or are being placed in the foster-adoption system. Not only do adopted children have a relationship with their parents, they have had brothers or sisters who have been allies, playmates, protectors, quasi-parents, or in some cases, involved in the abuse. Talking about the importance of sibling relationships often helps adoptive parents make the leap into considering contact with the birth family. Tom Rutherford thinks we need to be able to say to adoptive parents, "Yes, I know you want this 2-year old child, but this child has three siblings and they have grown up with each other. They will always be this child's family, no matter what kind of legal arrangement changes the parenting responsibilities. Taking a child into your home should mean acknowledging and honoring that child's unique history of relationships."

The Wilsons and Their Three Adopted Children

Samantha and Jerry have three children from the foster-adoption system. The couple turned to public adoption because they knew that there were thousands of children in the United States who needed stable and loving homes. Neither had a burning desire to have biological kids, and they had met several people who experienced successful public adoptions. They ultimately adopted three children: Adam, adopted at age 3, is now 15, and Alice and Jacob, who are full siblings and were adopted together as a sibling pair. Alice was adopted at age 4 and is now 11, and Jacob was adopted at age 2 and is now 9. They have dealt with some of the challenges of adopting children from the public system, but have identified ways to keep connected while maintaining good boundaries (interview, 2004).

Samantha Wilson, Adoptive Mother

It made perfect sense to me to try to keep in contact with whatever healthy family the kids had. Those of us who aren't adopted are blessed with that connection, and we often take it for granted. Just knowing

We need to change the system in many ways, and stop looking at the end of the legal adoption process as "finalization." The child may have a permanent home, but our job is not over.

— Susan Quash-Mah, Teamwork for Children

my extended family had given me a sense of myself as part of something bigger, not just me out here all alone. When we read Adam's adoption paperwork, we realized that he had a biological sister who was being adopted by another family. We had very little information about his birth parents, so we knew that his sister would be especially important to him. His birth mother had relinquished both of her children voluntarily because she was living on the edge and knew she couldn't take care of the kids. We hold her in our family by talking about how difficult it must have been for her. When Adam was younger and his baby-sitter turned 17, we pointed out to Adam that she was the same age his birth mother was when she decided she was unable to be a good parent. He really understood that.

Adam and his sister were in foster care together, and the foster mother had a good-bye party when Adam was placed with us. That was how we met his sister and her new adoptive parents. *The social services department decided that these siblings would be separated, but they never did anything to help our two families stay connected. There was never any conversation about the importance of maintaining sibling ties.* The other adoptive family lived close to us, and we were been able to get together three or four times a year. They have since moved out of the state, and Adam has flown to their new home independently for several summers. I cannot imagine my son not connecting with his biological sister—it just is part of who he is. His sister and her family are not *like* extended family, they *are* extended family.

Our next two kids were a whole different story. Alice and Jacob were in a foster-adopt situation because their birth parents were trying to rehabilitate after years of drug use. The birth parents were addicted to speed, and the birth grandparents were the ones who had called Child Protective Services. That must have been one of the hardest decisions they ever had to make—to call the police on their own child. These kids have gone through a lot of trauma, and Alice was afraid of the police because of the many times they came to the door to arrest her parents. She used to cry whenever her baby dolls were taken away, because when they were evicted and locked out of their apartment, she would lose all her dolls and other toys.

We had supervised visits with the birth parents during the first few months of the foster placement. I would drop the kids off with the social worker, and try to avoid contact with the birth parents, but I had to live with the consequences of those visits. Alice would regress afterwards, with serious tantrums and the loss of the toilet training she had established. Eventually, with the help of the social worker and the psychologist, we convinced the court that these kids were being too

> *I cannot imagine my son not connecting with his biological sister—it just is part of who he is. His sister and her family are not like extended family, they are extended family.*
>
> — Samantha, an adoptive mother of three children

negatively impacted by seeing their birth parents, and the court stopped the visits.

I wanted to honor the birth grandparents who had fought so hard to get these kids into a decent home. We began to see the paternal birth grandparents every other month, and continued for three years until the birth father and birth mother moved back in with his parents. The birth grandparents wanted to give their son and daughter-in-law another chance, because they had stopped using speed, and the birth father now had a job. Nevertheless, it didn't feel right for us to have visits when the birth father was so early in the recovery process. I want my kids to feel emotionally safe as well as physically safe, so my husband and I decided to not visit them until the birth father was in recovery for quite awhile. We have continued a sense of continuity with their early childhood through our connection with their foster parents. They love these kids and act as another set of grandparents, taking them for an occasional weekend when we need a break.

What has helped us most is that we are clear about our boundaries. When Jacob, our youngest, was having difficulty in school, we decided to put him ahead a grade because he is really smart. It was an anxiety-ridden period for us. We decided that we would not be in phone contact with his birth grandparents during this time because I knew that if I talked to them, they would be worried about how he was doing in his new situation. I didn't want to involve them in the drama. Even though they are extended family, it works best if we keep some separation.

On the other hand, when Adam was having trouble in school, one of my best sounding boards was his biological sister's adoptive mom. While her adoptive mother didn't have the same issues with Adam's sister, it was comforting to know she understood. We came to realize how hard we needed to advocate for our kids, particularly in the public school system. Even though my husband and I were very involved parents, our son still managed to get lost in "the system" and he failed middle school. We were thrilled to find a treatment program to address his needs, and he is now succeeding both socially and in school.

Looking back, I realize it would have been much better if the adoption professionals had facilitated a meeting between the two sets of adoptive parents for Adam and his sister. It has turned out great, but only because we were willing to figure out how to keep connections on our own. Not one of the adoption professionals we worked with helped us with a plan or even suggested that it would be good for the kids! When adoptees have siblings, the system should try to keep them together, and if they cannot do so, adoptive families should be asked if they are willing to stay in contact. Siblings are a huge part of adopted children's identity. For the most part, foster-adopt kids have lost their birth mother and their birth father, and if all they have is a sibling, you'd better try to keep in contact with them.

Two Dads, Nathan and Daniel, and Their Three Adopted Children: Defying Stereotypes

Nathan and Daniel are raising three children adopted through the public foster-adoption system. Benjamin was adopted at age 5 and is now 13, and the other two children were adopted at ages 8 and 2 and are now 11 and 5. Openness made sense to Nathan and Daniel from the beginning, but they have also grown wiser about how to protect their kids from being disappointed by their birth parents (interview, 2004).

Nathan and Daniel

Daniel remembers his first introduction to open adoption:

> One of the adoption training classes that struck me was the picture of a child-centered web of connections to others in the foster-adopt system. They showed the social worker, the foster parents, the birth parents, and the adoptive family. We liked that idea because when you are getting a child that child is not divorced from a whole set of relationships. Even if those relationships are severed legally, they are part of the children's identity. As a gay couple, our lives have always been about creating different kinds of family, and open adoption is just another part of that. But I have to admit it is a little odd—it is not like there is a template for hanging out with your kid's birth parents.

The idea of openness clicked for Nathan too. "We took the weblike connections to heart, and felt that we should trace all the important relationships our kids had that preceded us, and see what we could do to preserve them. Both of us being of mixed race is also another part of the equation, because there were a lot of mixed race children available." Their first son, Benjamin, was 5 years old when they adopted him, and Nathan and Daniel were aware of the many disruptions that he had already endured in his short life. Daniel recalls, "Meeting the foster parents that Benjamin had during a crucial time of his life deepened our understanding of keeping connections. They had put a lot of work into supporting the relationships between the kids and their birth families, and that made a big impression on us."

Recalling the early stages of negotiating contact visits, Daniel remembers, "Benjamin's birth mother loved him and was dedicated to having contact, but like we all are, she was utterly fallible. Sometimes she couldn't come through, promises were broken, and it was difficult for her to get around, especially as she had more children." Nathan adds, "Benjamin definitely

Siblings are a huge part of adopted children's identity. For the most part, foster-adopt kids have lost their birth mother and their birth father, and if all they have is a sibling, you'd better try to keep in contact with them.

— Samantha, an adoptive mother

went through some changes in the first year after placement, and had some problems with regression after our visits with his birth mother. Eventually, he wasn't so keen on seeing her so often, especially after we adopted our next child, who became his brother in our home."

Daniel laughs and remembers a story that illustrates some of the issues involved in transitioning to a family where there are new siblings.

> Something happened on one of our visits that showed us what was going on for Benjamin. We were visiting his birth mother and she had gotten a large fish tank. She was very excited about it and said to Benjamin, "Look, there is a fish for all of us" as she pointed to a fish for each of the three children who still lived with her, and one for Benjamin. Then Benjamin asked, "So, where is the fish for my brother in my new family?" When Benjamin realized that his birth mother hadn't put a fish in for the brother in his adoptive family, he turned his back on the tank and never looked back. It was as though he was saying, "If my new brother was not in that tank, I don't want anything to do with it." That showed us that Benjamin had made important steps in the transition to our family, and his brother here was as important to him as the siblings who remained with his birth mother.

Benjamin's birth mother has often taken the initiative to get in touch, but has been less consistent with honoring special days like birthdays and Christmas. "Neither she nor the gifts she said she would be sending, made an appearance for his birthday," Daniel says. "But I was proud that Benjamin could acknowledge that his feelings were hurt by saying, 'I can live with my Mom being a promise breaker. I don't like it, but that is what my Mom does, and that is one of the reasons that she can't take care of me.' Benjamin's brother has also dealt with disappointments with his birth mother, and it seemed like they were able to compare notes."

Daniel recalls one time that was particularly hard:

> Our second son's birth mother was planning a visit and I made it a big deal by saying, "What is the menu going to be, and how are we going to make this a really special dinner for your birth mom?" So we did all this planning and the day arrived, and we waited, and waited, and waited. She didn't show up or call. I felt bad about having made it a big deal, but the kids were really clear that they'd had enough of the big disappointments, and they were not going to count on her in the future. We helped them express their feelings, and began to set better boundaries to protect them from unnecessary hurt.

Nathan and Daniel share strong ideas about the forces that have affected the lives of their kids, and continue to affect their birth parents:

We understand what some of the forces are that have been exerted on these birth families. They are underprivileged people, and have had few resources to cope with the complexities of their lives. This helps us understand them and continue to try to find ways to keep the connection.

— Nathan, adoptive father

We both have a very strong sense of our own power as people. We are not in the closet in any area of our lives, and we are empowered by our own personal histories. Our family defies stereotypes: while at the same time we are two gay men of color, we recognize that we are also relatively privileged. We both are professionals, and both of us have a graduate education, but we also know where we have come from. We understand what some of the forces are that have been exerted on these birth families. They are not bad people, they are underprivileged people, and have had few resources to cope with the complexities of their lives. This helps us understand them and continue to try to find ways to keep the connection.

CHAPTER 7

Opening Closed Adoptions

Many birth and adoptive families did not start off with a relationship to each other. Either they worked with adoption professionals who were not supportive of openness, they did not embrace openness themselves, or they were not informed about the range of possibilities available to them. Many birth parents returned to communities that were not supportive of their maintaining contact, or they were living with parents who discouraged keeping in touch with the adoptive family. Some adoptive parents were able to meet birth parents, but within the first year or two, contact was gradually broken off. This chapter will look at some of the concerns about opening closed and semi open adoptions, the effects on the child, their siblings, the birth and adoptive parents, and the practices that will help the process go more smoothly. Then we will hear the stories of two families who opened their children's adoptions. One of the adoptive mothers acknowledges that openness has made their lives richer and more complex, and as she says, "I wouldn't change a thing."

Concerns About Opening the Relationship

Many factors may contribute to birth and adoptive parents taking the steps toward opening a closed or semi-open adoption. Years of actual parenting have helped adoptive parents feel fully entitled to claim the child as their own, and they no longer see birth parents as a threat to their sense of family. Other families have experienced the benefits of openness with the adoption of a second child, and reconsider opening the relationship for their first child. Other adoptive families are moved by the expressed need of their children to know more about their origins. Ruth McRoy and Harold Grotevant (1998) report that two thirds of fully disclosed adoptions did not start out that way. This means that many families are opening adoptions when their children are older.

Beth, an adoptive mom remembers, "From an early age, my daughter expressed a strong interest in hearing more about her birth mother. It was as though she needed to be told this story over and over again, as she struggled to understand what had happened. By the time she was 4, she would ask if her birth mother was sick, or if she was still alive, and when could we see her. I knew that we needed to try to fill in the gaps."

Carol Demuth, a counselor and educator at Buckner Adoption and Maternity Services in Texas, sees the same need in older adopted children. "Ten to 17-year-old kids from semi-open adoptions are coming back to us in droves. Some are having a hard time and they are asking for increased contact, some have questions about their origins, and some desperately want a photograph" (interview, 2005). Often these are happy and well adjusted children who are very attached to their adoptive family. Their longing to know more of who they are is a natural part of being an adopted person, not a sign of maladjustment.

These are happy and well-adjusted children who are very attached to their adoptive family. Their longing to know more about who they are is a natural part of being an adopted person, not a sign of mal-adjustment.

Once they decide to open a closed adoption, adoptive parents have some of the same questions that people do when they consider openness from the beginning of the child's life. How much contact is appropriate? What role will we have in determining the relationship? Will our child be faced with another rejection if a birth parent is not able to maintain a healthy connection? Guidance from an experienced adoption professional is especially important at this stage since family and friends may be strong counselors against developing relationships with birth parents. An adoptive grandmother might feel even more threatened than the adoptive parents by the introduction of a birth grandmother into the family.

Adoptive parents may have formed assumptions and judgments about the birth parents based on what they were like during the crisis of the unplanned pregnancy. They will need to adjust to different people who might have moved on to create families of their own. Dealing with their child's full or half siblings may raise concerns about how to integrate these relationships into their lives. Most of all, they will need to be especially vigilant to the adopted child's questions and concerns as they begin this process.

Birth parents have their own unique concerns. Some may still be experiencing lingering emotional pain, even if they do not regret the decision. For some, the adoption itself may have been a destabilizing event from which they have not yet recovered. Others may have married and had additional children, and are concerned about the effects on their new family. Some have partners or children who have never been told about the adoption, and others have family members who are opposed to including the adoptive family in their lives. Many birth parents had to maintain a certain level of secrecy within their own families about the adoption, and opening it could compromise some of those relationships. One of the biggest challenges that birth parents have to face is not having been able to raise a particular child. Seeing the child and realizing all the growth and development that has been missed, may bring up new waves of grief, guilt, or regret.

Tools to Help

It is easy for the adults involved to get caught up in the exhilaration and tension of the reunion, but adoptive parents need to stick to the goal of helping their child or teen establish a positive relationship with the birth parents. Patricia Martinez Dorner, an adoption educator and counselor, specializes in opening closed adoptions. She is the author of *Talking to Your Child about Adoption*, *How to Open an Adoption*, and she is the coauthor with Kathleen Silber, of *Children of Open Adoption*:

> The process needs to be opened up in a way that is manageable for everyone, and great care should be taken not to proceed to the next step until all parties are comfortable. There is no magic in opening closed adoptions. Building trust takes years, and reconnecting is only one step in that process. Birth and adoptive parents need to look at their expectations and fears, and carefully examine each of them" (interview, 2004).

Don't wait until your kid is already having problems before you consider opening the relationship.

— Ellen, adoptive mother of Juliana

In Melina and Roszia (1993), the authors suggest having a Vision Matching Session to help each party discuss their new roles, examine how opening the adoption will change the relationships, and decide about contact and how conflicts will be settled. "If a child is old enough to understand, make sure he has the opportunity to voice his fears and anxieties in a counseling session. If the child is old enough to have an opinion, respect that opinion" (pages 217–218). Sometimes the adoptive and birth parents may be anxious to meet each other, but the child is not ready to take that leap. "Parents should not press a relationship on a child until he is ready. Adoptees historically, have not been allowed control of their destiny, so allow the child some say in this relationship" (page 218).

Each family needs to decide what is right for them, but it is important to remember that although it is never too late to open a relationship, it is often best to do it before the roller coaster of the teenage years. As Ellen, an adoptive mother, says in one of this chapter's profiles, "Don't wait until your kid is already having problems before you consider opening the relationship." Pacing requires not proceeding until each member of the adoption triad is comfortable, but going too slow may bog down the process. Opening an adoption in the early years allows the child to grow up in the open adoption, developing relationships gradually. This might be preferable to entering into a relationship during the teenage years, when there are so many other challenging issues between the teenager and the adoptive parent.

Adoptive parents may have the fear that if their kids are in touch with their birth parents, they may gravitate toward them, especially during the rebellious teenage years. Patricia Martinez Dorner is adamant about this point:

> My message to adoptive parents is this: when children can fill in parts of themselves, they will become more whole, not less yours. When families are trying to open a closed adoption with younger children, the process is totally guided by the parents. But when the process begins when kids are in their teens, the teens must also be part of it from the very beginning. I warn adoptive parents that they still need to be in charge, even if their child is older. Although they may want to turn responsibility over to their teenager in other matters, it is not sound to do that in regards to opening adoptions. As adults, it is our job to develop and support these relationships, even into young adulthood (interview, 2004).

Birth parents are presented with other major challenges when an adoption is opened. They will need to accept that the child is not the same as the infant they relinquished, but an entirely different person. Ms. Dorner underlines the issues that birth parents need to address if they are to be successful:

> Many birth mothers are often hesitant to participate because they have such a fear of re-experiencing the grief. I let them know that if you walk through this grief, you can be an important part of this child's life. Some birth parents may not be able to open things up without risking the loss of support from other family members. It takes a lot to turn away from those that supported you in your adoption decision and then open it up years later. Birth parents also need to understand that it is not only for this child, but for all of her subsequent children. When grieving is unfinished or unresolved, the attachment to future children can be affected. Birth parents need to know that whatever they do, they will always be important to the child that they created. They can be a "ghost" figure or a personal resource, and they need help in deciding which one they want to be (interview, 2004).

Birth parents need to know that whatever they do, they will always be important to the child that they created. They can be a "ghost" figure or a personal resource, and they need help in deciding which one they want to be.

— Patricia Martinez Dorner

Sibling Issues

Opening a closed adoption will impact all members of the birth and adoptive family, including the siblings, and it is important to consider their needs too. Siblings of the adopted child or teen might be introduced to full or half siblings in the birth family, and their own feelings of jealousy, competition, or familial loyalty may need to be addressed. Juliana, profiled later in this chapter, was involved in opening her own adoption. She remembers one of the joint family meetings: "I had an older brother in my adoptive family, and he met my younger brother in my birth family when we reunited. When my newly found brother referred to me as his sister, I could see the shocked look on the face of my brother from my adoptive family: like 'why are *you* calling *my* sister, sister?'"

Siblings who remained in the birth family, or who were born after a child was relinquished, may have difficult feelings about this new member of their extended family. "How come so much attention is going toward her? Is she somehow more important than we are? If you gave her away, might that happen to us someday? Now that we have found her, can she come and live with us?" When visits occur with the adoptive families, obvious differences in socioeconomic class may be an issue for some siblings. "How come my half-sister has her own computer in her room? How come she has so much stuff that I don't?" Opening the adoption may bring up so much unresolved grief for a birth parent that children in the home may become angry and resentful with the adopted sibling, or the adoptive family, for making their mother so unhappy.

Children in birth and adoptive families will need to be reminded about why the adoption took place, and why it is being opened up at this time. Younger siblings in the adoptive family may need to be reassured that they are not going to lose their brother or sister, or be loved any less. It might be helpful to have older siblings talk about their concerns about the effects of reunion on their relationship with their siblings and their parents. It is important to convey to all of the siblings that the child or teen may have many strong feelings about meeting a biological relative for the first time. All siblings in both the birth and adoptive families should be assured that even though they might be expanding to include new people, their relationships within their own family are primary and will remain so.

Making Use of Professionals

Birth and adoptive parents are as human as any other set of parents, and will make mistakes, will not pay enough attention to every member of the family, and will occasionally be confused about the right choices to make. Being honest, not proceeding to the next step until they are ready, and getting help if they need assistance is the best guide. "Opening closed adoptions is not a cure-all, but it gives children possibilities of loving relationships that answer many of their questions, and can lessen acting out and other troubling behaviors. Both birth and adoptive parents need to face their fears in the process, and then they usually come through it with greater confidence about their roles, and greater empathy for the feelings of the child" (Dorner, interview, 2004).

Reading books, joining support groups, or seeking professional assistance can help smooth the process. Not discussing these important issues can

Opening closed adoptions is not a cure-all, but it gives children new possibilities of loving relationships that answer many of their questions, and can lessen acting out and other troubling behaviors.

— Patricia Martinez Dorner

make the difference between a reunion that works and one that doesn't. The following story is of Josephia, a 17-year-old who was still in high school when she became pregnant.

Josephia chose adoption because she didn't have the emotional or financial resources to raise a child at that point in her life. After locating an adoption facilitator who supported openness, she chose a couple that seemed receptive to having contact. Unfortunately, the discussions about contact were vague, and left the impression that the adoptive parents would remain in touch, but they didn't spell out what that might look like.

During the first few years, the adoptive parents rarely made contact, but Josephia thought that they just needed time to get used to the new baby. She thought it was best to wait and see what happened. This is a position that many birth mothers find themselves in: waiting for the adoptive parents to take the initiative. "It did not feel like my place to push for anything more than they were willing to give." After several attempts, she was finally able to get a few pictures of her birth son. "I was so relieved to see those photos, but several years went by with no contact except an occasional letter."

When her birth son was 7 years old, Josephia felt a strong need to see him, and after much hesitation, she wrote the adoptive family. They responded positively, and she was surprised when they offered a visit. On the day of the visit, Josephia felt it was going well considering that she and the adoptive parents did not really know each other, and hadn't talked about what they wanted or expected from the visit. Josephia felt joyful that they were finally connecting and her birth son seemed to relish being with her. When it was time for her to say good-bye, her birth son had a completely unanticipated major tantrum, throwing himself about like a 3-year-old. Josephia remembers, "His parents seemed totally shocked and overwhelmed at the extent of his distress. He clearly was having a hard time saying good-bye to me, and neither he, nor I, nor his parents, knew how to help him handle his feelings." At that point, Josephia was rushed out of the door.

When Josephia returned home, she felt shell-shocked. The visit had gone very well until the last minute, and she was fearful that the tantrum would make it hard for the adoptive family to continue contact. "I cried for weeks because I felt torn apart knowing that he had such a hard time. I kept wondering if there was anything I could have done to make it easier." When she finally called the adoptive family, their number was disconnected. She has not been able to make contact since that fateful visit, which was over four years ago. What started out as a hopeful reconnection ended with a painfully opened wound.

If these families had received adequate preparation in resuming their relationship, they might have met each other before including the son.

Incremental steps of communication between the birth mother and son with cards, letters, or phone calls might have been helpful. Most importantly, these families would have had a facilitated discussion to share their hopes and expectations about openness, and how they would deal with problems if they arose. Contrast this story with the following profiled families who made use of the open adoption literature, professional guidance, and facilitation. Keep in mind the following questions: For parents, what are some of the positive ways you might react if an adopted teen began to act out in anger towards you? What might a professional's role be in helping sort out what was an adoption issue and what was a normal developmental issue for the teenage years? What were the most important steps taken by the family profiled below when opening their adoption?

Opening a Closed Transracial Adoption with Guidance and Support

Juliana is now 22 years old. Opening her adoption was carefully paced and took place gradually over a several-year period with the assistance of two open adoption experts. The adoptive family had a first visit with Juliana's birth family when she was 15. Ellen, the adoptive mother of Juliana, is the coordinator of a democratic high school program where she is also a guidance counselor and an administrator:

Ellen, Adoptive Mother of Juliana

I considered myself an informed adoptive parent, and I am also a guidance counselor who works with teenagers, but I was still not prepared for the complexity and pain that adolescence presented for my daughter. When she was in her early teens, she started having a difficult time with depression and some acting out. It was clear that her self-esteem was being affected by not knowing more about who she was and where she came from. Juliana is Mexican-American and had few positive Latina role models at the time. We went to the Center for Family Connections where the director, Joyce Maguire Pavao, suggested that we consider opening the adoption. We felt we were not fully ready to do this, but it was clear that Juliana had to learn more about her background and her Hispanic identity. All of us, the birth and adoptive families, would have been much better off if my daughter had known much earlier who it was she looked like, and that her birth family loved her.

We were fortunate that we had at our disposal two of the best adoption experts in the country. In addition to meeting several times with Joyce Maguire Pavao, we turned to Patricia Dorner who is a skilled intermediary for opening closed adoptions. We had extensive

> *I considered myself an informed adoptive parent, but I was still not prepared for the complexity and pain that adolescence presented for my daughter.*
>
> — Ellen, adoptive mother of Juliana

facilitated conversations over the phone with Patricia's assistance. Because Juliana was a young teen, we made it clear that she was not doing this alone—it was something our whole family was doing together. We reinforced that philosophy by my always being on the other line when Juliana and her birth mother spoke on the phone. When we first communicated with the adoption agency, we discovered a letter that the birth mother had written to them two years after the adoption. She wanted to know how her daughter was doing, but that letter was never given to us. It was so painful to think of how she must have felt when she got no response. We would have been glad to have sent pictures and letters telling the birth mother how Juliana was doing. Why did she have to suffer for so long?

We went from finding the birth mother, which took several months, to letters, increasing phone calls, and then to arrangements to visit. Of course, I had some concerns: What if my daughter was disappointed? What if the birth mother was not able to stay in touch? But we took these steps over a three-year period under Patricia's guidance, and moved forward only when everyone was ready. We discovered that our daughter's birth mother was ashamed about the adoption, and was worried about meeting us. Patricia helped her understand that we were doing this for Juliana's benefit, and that we didn't feel negatively about her at all. The supportive dialogue helped her see that she could have an important and valuable role to play in Juliana's life.

Juliana wanted desperately to know who she looked like, whose personality resembled her own, and that she was loved. All of this and more was accomplished by opening her adoption. She is a healthy 22-year-old now with a positive identity as a Hispanic young woman. I marvel at her maturity as she is well adjusted and has a close relationship with her father, her brother, and me. She is very happy in college where she hopes to major in holistic psychology and counseling. We have direct contact with the birth family through phone calls, e-mails, and visits once a year. Her extended Mexican-American family has welcomed us into their midst, and we have met grandparents, aunts, and uncles and three half siblings! We never felt threatened by the birth family, only grateful for their willingness to get to know us, and their acceptance of us as extended family.

My advice about opening closed adoptions is to go slowly, check on how each of you is doing, and respect the other family and their values. I cannot emphasize enough how important it was to have had experienced professionals helping us through the entire process. As adoptive families you should try to remember that you are meeting an entire birth family, rather than just introducing one child to his or her birth parent. Becoming extended family will affect everyone, including your other children. But most of all, remember that more than anything else, your child cares about being loved and knowing who it is she looks like. For adoptive parents, I can tell you that that no one replaces you as the parents, but that there can be room in your hearts for all kinds of love (interview, 2004).

Juliana, Adoptee, Speaking at Age 19

When I was growing up, I didn't want people to know I was adopted. I used to make up stories to explain my features. People would ask my Mom or me what I was. I didn't know where I came from so I didn't know how to answer them. I think my parents knew I felt lost, but they had no idea how bad I was actually feeling. I began to beat myself up inside, and grew angrier and more resentful toward my parents. I remember one time at a restaurant with many members of my mother's extended family. We were fooling around and a cousin asked the waiter if he could tell which kids belonged to which family. I felt like a total outcast. I knew I didn't look like I belonged to anyone. I had never had that feeling of looking like I belonged, and I desperately wanted it.

When I was about 12, my mother was going through some adoption papers and noticed that my name and my birth mom's name were whited out. She asked a secretary at work if there was a way to take the whiteout off, but save what was underneath. She knew I was "having issues" so she wanted to help. When she was finally able to tell me what my name was at birth, I could no longer lie to myself about having been adopted. I couldn't split myself up into someone who denied I was adopted, and someone who was obsessed about who I was. Now I absolutely had to find out more about who I was.

This eventually sent me into a depression, and I was angry most of the time. My mother and I fought a lot because I tested her in a million ways. I put my parents through hell and back during this period—doing everything I could to push them away. It was almost as though I was trying to convince them that I was unlovable, and test them to see if they would leave me. Deep inside, I knew they weren't going anywhere, but I felt like they had to prove it again and again. I think my Mom always understood that this had something to do with adoption. We finally had counseling with Joyce Maguire Pavao, and help preparing for the search from Patricia Dorner. They didn't talk to me like a teenager with "adoption issues." They explained everything to me: the steps, how I might feel, and predicting the ups and downs of the process. It was really important to me that it felt like everyone in the family was helping move this along, not just me.

Remember that more than anything else, your child cares about being loved and knowing who she looks like. For adoptive parents, I can tell you that that no one replaces you as the parents, but that there can be room in your hearts for all kinds of love.

— Ellen, adoptive mother of Juliana

Finally after almost a year of talking about our feelings, Patricia found my birth mother. It was strange to talk to her because she sounded different from what I expected, but it helped me to have that contact. We exchanged letters and phone calls for almost three years before my whole family flew out to meet her the summer before my senior year. I was calm the entire trip, but as we waited in the motel room, she called to say she would be a few minutes late. That's when I panicked. I was sweating and having a hard time breathing because I felt so anxious. I thought I couldn't go through with it, but my Dad helped me calm down. When my Mom opened the door, I was in shock. My birth mom cried, my Mom cried, but all I could do was sit there and stare at her. I thought that she would look like me, but she didn't. Over the next three days, we met my great grandmother, my grandmother, two brothers, a sister, and we immediately connected as brothers and sisters. I didn't have too many issues about the fact that my birth mom had kept several children but did not feel she could raise me. The next year, they stayed at our house and came to my high school graduation. This has met a lot of my needs to know who I am.

When I was younger, I had some Hispanic friends whose house I would go to. I remember wanting more of the food and culture. My parents did a good job of exposing me to Latin culture. We traveled to Mexico and Spain, and they encouraged me to take Spanish, but meeting my birth family has made me even more proud to be Hispanic. It helped a side of me to come out even more. I know that if I had been given the option of connecting to my birth family when I was younger, I wouldn't have felt so lost. It's the little things, like whose eyes do I have, that really matter. It is so important—you don't know what life is like without it. Not knowing these little things can build and build until you are lost inside. I feel so different as a person now that I know who I am.

Meeting my birth family has made me even more proud to be Hispanic. It helped a side of me to come out even more. I know that if I had been given the option of connecting to my birth family when I was younger, I wouldn't have felt so lost.

— Juliana, an adoptee, speaking at age 19

A Rich and Complex Life: A Blended, Multiracial, Adoptive Family

Gail and her husband live on the East Coast, where they have two biological sons, ages 22 and 20, and two daughters through adoption: Alisha, age 14, and Beth, age 11. Their family represents a myriad of overlapping issues in adoption: they are a blended family of both biological and adopted children; they are a multicultural and transracial family; they started out with closed adoptions and opened them when their children were older; and they have different degrees of contact with each of their daughters' birth families. Like other adoptive families, openness has made their lives richer, but also much more complex, but as Gail says, "I wouldn't change a thing" (interview, 2003).

While reading the profile, adoption professionals might keep in mind the following questions: how would you assist an adoptive parent who felt bad about the grief that a birth parent was feeling? How would you support a birth parent if a child continued to express anger about the relinquishment? How would you assist an adoptive father in determining what his role would be in maintaining a relationship with his child's birth parents?

Gail, Adoptive Mother of Alisha and Beth

I always knew I wanted openness in our adoptions because of reading adoption books, especially Betty Jean Lifton (1994) who talks so movingly about what it feels like to be adopted. The agencies we worked with did not allow openness, but we hoped that we could find a way to communicate with the birth family. I knew that openness would give our daughters their priceless birthright—the one thing I would never be able to give them.

We had to search for both of my daughters' birth families, and we did so when the girls were 5 and 7. My oldest daughter, Alisha, had a rocky beginning with several foster placements and intermittent contact with her birth mother until she was 3 months old, when she was adopted by us. From the time she was 2, I could see signs of her mourning for her birth mother. She was also dealing with the experience of being African American in a mostly white community. Her birth mother is from a close-knit family, several of whom live in the same geographical area. Although we took steps to include African Americans as our friends, and changed to a more diverse church, we still lived in a mostly white neighborhood. Alisha always seemed particularly aware of the differences between herself and other kids at preschool.

When she was two and a half, she was playing underneath a table when a visitor asked where her birth mother lived. I said I didn't know. Alisha must have overheard this, and that night she woke up crying, saying that her mommy was lost. I knew that she was not talking about me. I realized then that we would eventually need to open up the adoption. By the time my daughter was 4, she was both happy and sad most of the time. Happy with most of her life, her older brothers, her little sister, but just below that was a layer of sadness and insecurity that was never far from the surface. We knew we had to open the adoption.

She soon began sending more signals about wanting to know her birth mother. I remember us reading a book together about a girl wondering what her life would have been like if she had stayed in her country of origin. After reading this, Alisha started crying, "That little

By the time my daughter was 4, she was both happy and sad most of the time. Happy with most of her life, but just below that was a layer of sadness and insecurity that was never far from the surface. We knew we had to open the adoption.

— Gail, an adoptive mother

girl knows more about where she came from than I do." She actually came right out and said, "I don't want to hurt your feelings, but I need my birth mother." I didn't take it personally because all the adoption books are very clear about this. I knew Alisha didn't want to go and live somewhere else—she just wanted to know more about who she was. We began our search with the Internet, and with the help of a member of Concerned United Birth Parents (CUB).

When Alisha was 7, we decided to seek professional help, and went to one of the best: Joyce Maguire Pavao at the Center for Family Connections in Massachusetts. She helped us write a letter to Alisha's birth mother that included photos. When we finally made the first phone contact with Alisha's birth mother, whose name is Mary, I told her that my daughter needed to know her. We had no way to call her back, and we did not hear from her again for over two years. Finally, we sent another letter to her via her sisters and soon after, she called and we arranged to meet for the first time without my daughter. When she approached us with her sisters, I knew immediately which one was Mary. We liked her immediately, and I had visions of our becoming one big happy family.

It was invaluable to have help sorting out everyone's feelings about the sudden openness. My husband, Mary, and myself met with Joyce Maguire Pavao, and came away with a clearer understanding of our feelings and expectations, plus a reminder of who we were doing this for. Joyce explained to Mary that *all* of our children were now related to her, by being siblings of Alisha, and that it was important for her to have some kind of relationship with all of them. Mary has been scrupulous in taking this advice and has warmly embraced all our children.

Alisha has always had a strong intuitive sense and one night she said, "I wonder what my birth mother is thinking right now." I said that I thought her birth mother was very happy, and told her about our meeting. Three weeks later, Alisha met Mary for the first time. I remember seeing my daughter walk down the street with her birth mother: they had the same walk and the same build. I had been seeing my daughter separated from a part of herself for so long. Now when I look at her, I can clearly see that she is a much happier child, she feels so much more complete.

Mary and I were ready for more contact than my daughter was so we had to slow things down to match the pace of a 7-year-old who needed time to sort out her difficult feelings. Alisha didn't want to return to her birth mom, but she was angry about having been relinquished. During that first year, she called her birth mom several days a week, even though she often had nothing to say. Mary tolerated this, but it was difficult for her to have been reunited with her child after years of grieving, and then have the child be angry or distant. After two years of getting close and then dancing away, Alisha was finally able to let go of the anger, and develop a lovely relationship with her birth mom and her family. She was a bridesmaid in her birth mom's wedding.

My biggest challenge has been dealing with Mary's grief in the first years of the reunion. I wished there was something I could do that would lessen the pain she was feeling. I finally realized that there was nothing I could do, and that Mary would take care of her pain when she was ready. I was in a hurry for her to get to a place *I* thought was better, because I didn't like living with the knowledge that she was hurting so much. So I was making it about me, and of course it was not about me.

Over time, Mary and her husband's relationship to us has changed, and now we are close to both of them. They renewed their wedding vows and our whole family was part of the ceremony. Of course, there have been some misunderstandings that we needed to sort out. In the beginning, Mary's family wanted to see my daughter frequently, but Alisha was not ready. In their family, children would not have had the right to pace something like this, so they did not understand our hesitancy, and they felt hurt by it. The changes in my daughter's birth mother since the reunion are unbelievable. Her sadness and grief have transformed into strength and determination. Mary says that her life got better the day we found her. It was also the day Alisha's life got better and because of that, our entire family "got better."

Relationships with our other daughter's birth family have proven to be more difficult. Our daughter Carol was the youngest of three children, and she shares the same birth parents with two brothers who are being raised by the birth mother. When the boys found out about Carol they were devastated at having missed so much time with her. Carol's brothers mean the world to her, and that is why the relationship is so important to us. But there are times when I don't feel like reaching out, because it is almost always our family that has to do the reaching. There are major differences between our families in access to resources, and the birth parents live close to the margins. When they visit us, we pay for the tickets, which makes the power imbalance even greater. But even with these difficulties, we are glad that we opened the adoption.

Carol's birth mom has not been ready to tell her entire family about our daughter, so when we visit, we are kept secret from some family members. The sadness and the regret her birth mother feels is still a problem. When we return from these visits, I am exhausted because I feel as if I am taking care of everyone. I have encouraged her to find

The changes in my daughter's birth mother since the reunion are unbelievable. Her sadness and grief have transformed into strength and determination.

— Gail,
adoptive mother of
Alisha and Beth

someone who can help her with her feelings, but it is not in her nature to use counselors. Carol is sometimes hurt because her birth family is less involved with us than Alisha's birth family. Yet, Carol loves the visits, and she spends most of the time with her brothers.

The biggest challenge for me was to accept that I couldn't alleviate the emotional pain of either of my daughter's birth mothers. In the past, I have encouraged them to seek out emotional help, but it wasn't my place to do that, and I can see that now. Feeling guilty about the birth mother's grief will not help them or you. It is important to remember that you need to take care of the other people in your own family at the same time you are nurturing the reunions. We have two sons who were in their teens during the reunions, and it was quite intense. Although they understood, they sometimes felt their own issues were tossed aside. What kept us sane and focused was getting professional help. Don't do this alone!

I initiate most of the contact between the families, and there are times when I have rebelled against this role, feeling that I was doing more than my share. But until these relationships normalize, someone has to be the conductor to make sure the ball is not dropped. Don't wait to open the adoption, especially if your child is asking about her birth family. If we had waited until our daughter was 18, it would have been too late. Before the teen years, your children are not yet revolting against you. That means that they can accept comfort from you during the process, and don't have to make you the villain.

There is no question that openness complicates family life, but there has never been a time when I wished it had not happened. Connections with our daughter's birth families have changed all of us, including our sons. The thing that keeps these relationships going is knowing that this is what our children need. If they were diabetic, I would give them insulin. If they loved basketball, I would do my best to give them an opportunity to play. If they are adopted, they need to know and have contact with their birth families. Our children now feel complete, and they project an air of confidence and maturity that is noticeable to everyone who meets them. Open adoption is a promise to put the child at the center of whatever you do.

Open adoption is a promise to try to do your best, a promise not to let the relationships falter if you can help it, a promise to put the child at the center of whatever you do.

— Gail, an adoptive mother

Alisha at Age 13

Before we opened my adoption, I was mad because I didn't get why I was put up for adoption. All of my friends knew who their parents were, and it didn't feel fair that I didn't know who *my* birth parents were. My Mom and Dad began to search when I was in second grade, and finally found my birth mother. My brother wasn't supposed to tell me, but he let me know when they were meeting her for the first time and later they showed me pictures of her. It was weird to see people who looked like me for the first time in my life. At first, I thought I wanted to have the same kind of relationship with my birth mother that I had with my parents. But after a few years, I realized that isn't really possible. My relationship with her is different—like a close friend and an older sister.

In the first year after we met I was still angry with my birth mom. I was mostly mad that I didn't get to stay with her from the beginning, even though I didn't want to live with her now. It's not as if I wanted to trade my parents in for her, it's just that I didn't like the idea that I was given away. I am not sure what I wanted from her, but I knew that I definitely wanted an apology. I wanted to hear her say she was sorry for what had happened.

We understand each other better now. I might still be a little mad occasionally, but mostly it is gone. As I have gotten older, I understand my birth mom more, and understanding her has made me realize that this was not about me—it was about her and the situation she was in. Knowing that directly from her has helped me a lot. My entire family was part of my birth mom's wedding, and I got to meet my whole extended birth family. It was great meeting all these people who knew who I was, and I got to see where I came from.

I have been shielded from having to deal with a lot of the race stuff because I was home schooled by my mother for many years, so I didn't go to the public school in our neighborhood that was mostly white. We know a lot of other mixed race families through our adoption community, and we belong to a diverse church where there are a lot of other kids and families like us. We have since moved to a more diverse and mixed community, and I feel even more at home.

My advice to birth and adoptive parents is that they should ask themselves how they would feel about not having an identity, not knowing where they came from. It's not fair to not know your parents. Knowing them makes me feel just like everyone else and I feel better about myself. If you had a choice, you would probably say yes to knowing more about who you are and I am glad my family has given me that choice.

Understanding my birth mother has made me realize that this was not about me—it was about her and the situation she was in. Knowing that directly from her has helped me a lot.

— Alisha, age 13

CHAPTER 8

Unique Families—
Unique Challenges

Openness presents unique challenges and opportunities. In this chapter, birth and adoptive family members recount their stories as they deal with a myriad of different issues: managing the logistics of multiple birth families, dealing with how and when to disclose adoption secrets, having children from both closed and open adoptions, and being in an open adoption with one's own best friend. These families answer the question: Will openness complicate your lives? Yes, they answer, it will, but it will complicate your lives in ways that add immeasurable depth and richness to you, your family, and your children.

These families' stories are not meant to be representative of those in open adoption. Each of them has created a truly unique arrangement that represents the participants' own personalities, preferences, capabilities, and resources. When I lead adoption support groups, I ask people to make an inventory of their emotional, spiritual, financial, and community assets, in order to make the best decision about the kind of adoption that will suit them. The resources available to any particular family involve much more than their financial assets. The term *resources* can include whether grandparents are available to help with child care, whether the public schools are adequate or whether the parents have to face tuition payments, or whether the parents' community has enough of a diverse population to support the ethnic and racial identity of a child in a transracial adoption. People need to make decisions based on what will work for them, not on what is possible for another family.

Looking back on their experiences, some of the families who are profiled here would have done things differently. They share their stories, because like most families, they have managed to deepen their open adoption relationships in spite of having problems along the way. They are sharing their stories to give us a realistic portrait of how openness has changed their lives.

There are a few questions before or after each interview, to help readers consider what their own preferences and capabilities might be. Birth and adoptive parents need to know when they can stretch beyond their comfort zone and when they cannot, and this kind of self-awareness is a vital part of what makes open adoption relationships work.

Dealing with Multiple Birth Families

Tom and Mary McNalley of Michigan have four children ranging in age from 2 to 10, all adopted through the same agency. They are all open adoptions so they have varying degrees of contact with eight different birth parents. Adoptive parents will want to carefully consider the challenges of maintaining open relationships with the birth families of several different children. Keep in mind the following questions as you read Mary's story: What kinds of boundaries were established and how? What additional boundaries might you need to create to make these relationships work for you (interview, 2004)?

Mary McNalley, Adoptive Mother of Four

Mary McNalley does not have a lot of time for interests other than her four children, but she does manage to take many photographs and create scrapbooks. She enjoys making digital movies of her family, adding music and graphics, and sharing them with the birth families:

The logistics are hard, but after the first year, the visits with each of the birth families have decreased to about two to three times a year. In the beginning, we talked with each of them about our fears of people dropping by unannounced. We explained what we needed in order to make this work, and they all have been respectful of that. All of our birth mothers and two of our birth fathers know each other, and use one another for support. When we gathered together for the first time as a large group, everyone was able to see how many people we have in our extended birth families—from great-grandparents down to the birth parents, and siblings or cousins. Many of them have made an effort to get to know these kids: several grandmothers have sent special handmade gifts, others send cards and include us in their own family reunions.

We have tried to help all of the birth parents understand that if a birth parent brings gifts, they need to do it for all of our kids. Although these kids are from four different birth families, they are all brothers and sisters in our family and need to be treated as such. We have had to politely ask one birth family to do this several times, but sometimes it takes awhile for people to change. A similar issue is having the birth family member snapping pictures of just their *own* birth child. The other children do not understand why that particular sibling is the current star.

If a birth parent brings gifts, they need to do it for all of our kids. Although these kids are from four different birth families, they are all brothers and sisters in our family and need to be treated as such. Adoption agencies could do a better job of explaining this to birth parents.

— Mary McNalley, adoptive mother of four children with open adoptions

Our children consider each sibling's birth parents as their relatives too, so all of them want to sit on the lap of the visiting birth parent. Adoption agencies could do a better job of explaining this to birth parents, so they heard it from another source besides us. It is difficult to be in the position of reminding birth families about basic issues like this, when they should have heard it from the adoption professionals.

This next issue is an unusual one and difficult to speak about, but I have heard other adoptive families talk about it so I know we are not alone. One of our birth parents has seemed especially concerned about her birth son's inevitable small injuries, asking probing questions about bumped lips or black eyes. Children are bound to have bumps and bruises, but it seems as if she is wondering if anything negative has happened. This particular birth mother may have had a history of abuse or neglect, and of course, is especially concerned about it. We have never spoken about this openly, but it's something that has been a challenge to overcome. Maybe we are more prone to thinking that the birth parents are questioning us, when they are actually just showing concern, but it does feel as if we are being scrutinized.

Openness sometimes adds a little extra pressure to be accountable to some of our birth families. We signed up one of our children for a free preschool program that does not have the best reputation, but with four kids, we need the financial break. It wouldn't change our decision, but we were concerned that the child's birth family would be disappointed. They had made it clear that education was very important to them, but if a decision is right for *us*, it must be made with *our* priorities in mind. We cannot make decisions to please the birth parents! We take our responsibility to our children, as well as their birth families seriously, which I think is good for all of us, but I occasionally wish that this feeling of accountability was not quite so strong.

In the beginning, I felt appreciation and gratitude to our kids' birth parents. Now I feel much more connected to them, not because they gave a child to us, but because they are related to our children. My feelings have shifted from feelings of gratitude, to feelings of respect and bonding. It's really something when you catch your child gesturing just like his birth parent—it can knock you off your feet sometimes. The genetic relationship is very powerful, and that alone can bring about feelings of great love for their birth families.

Since we adopted our first child, a lot has changed in the larger community. Years ago, some people thought we were crazy to do this, but they can now see how much these relationships have benefited these children. Our children are rooted in their identities, and they feel strengthened by having their birth parents in their lives. Just because

In the beginning, I felt appreciation and gratitude to our kids' birth parents. Now I feel much more connected to them, not because they gave a child to us, but because they are related to our children.

— Mary McNalley, adoptive mother of four children

we have a relationship with our children's birth family, doesn't mean that we don't feel secure as parents. You sit up enough nights with a sick child, and teach your children how to eat, count, ride a bike, and you will feel as secure as any parent does. Of course there are challenges in open adoptions, but even for us with four kids and their birth parents, they are far outweighed by the rewards.

The above account raises some interesting issues for birth and adoptive parents and the professionals who are working with them. How might the issue of accountability between birth and adoptive parents be explored? Is there a difference between respecting and honoring birth parents and being accountable to them? How would a professional handle the issue of birth parents who express particular concern about bruises and cuts?

Trying to Keep a Secret in an Open Adoption

Amy, Tom and Kristy, their daughter Samantha's birth mother, spent years trying to keep a secret about Samantha's full sibling who lived with the birth mother. The disclosure of that secret rocked their lives, but they have come through it with stronger relationships, deeper ties to each other, and a greater willingness to honor their roles in each other's lives (interview, 2003).

Amy, Adoptive Mother of Samantha and Julia

Amy is the mother of two, an avid reader who dabbles in travel, skiing, and chocolate. She gardens with her youngest daughter, shops with her big one, and makes the world a better place by working in health services.

After the birth of our daughter Samantha, my husband and I decided that our daughter's birth mother could initiate phone contact whenever she wanted to, and we would send letters and pictures about three times a year. It wasn't until Samantha was 10 that she expressed her desire to talk with her birth mother on the phone. We had all assumed that we would meet some day, but first we had to decide how to deal with the secret we had been keeping about Samantha's brother. Kristy had a son, Brandon, who was 14 months older than Samantha. An adoption group facilitator had urged us not to tell our daughter that she had a full sibling until both kids were teenagers or older. Looking back, that was a mistake that has caused a great deal of grief for our entire family.

When Samantha was 13, her birth mother called while we were not home, and blurted out something about Brandon. Samantha asked, "Brandon? Who is Brandon?" Kristy answered, "Your brother." Samantha quietly asked, "How old is he?" Kristy answered 14, at which point Samantha just said "Oh." We returned that night to a home that was radically different from the one we had left. Samantha was filled with rage. She had a brother that she didn't know about, and was furious that she could have been connecting to him all these years. Feeling betrayed, she wanted to know what other secrets had been kept from her.

Our whole family had been keeping this a secret for years, so everyone knew *except* Samantha. Kristy had been afraid that Brandon would never forgive her for the adoption, but when she finally told him, he took it surprisingly well. Soon he and Samantha started communicating, and when Brandon was close to his 16th birthday, Kristy invited us to a surprise party for him. When Kristy and Samantha saw each other for the first time, they stared as if they were looking into a mirror, and soon we were all crying. When Brandon walked in and saw Samantha he said, "Oh my God, it's you!" They were up for most of the night asking important questions about all the things that siblings would usually know about each other, like, "What kind of toothpaste do you use? What kind of cereal do you eat?"

Samantha's teen years have been especially hard. She was preoccupied with who she looked like in middle school and fantasized a lot about her birth mother. This was followed by the abrupt disclosure about having a brother, and then she dealt with my husband and me separating. Keeping this secret has proven to be the Achilles heel for our whole family. We said this was an open adoption, but we were creating a charade of openness as long as we kept this secret. I would advise birth and adoptive parents to tell the truth, even if it is painful and tell the truth before a kid is in his or her teens. The betrayal of our daughter's trust sent us all on a collision course that is still having an impact 3 years later. Kids can handle the truth much better than they can handle the betrayal of being lied to. All adopted children deserve this (interview, 2003).

Tom, Adoptive Father of Samantha and Julia

We knew that adoption was a win/lose proposition, and we thought that by maintaining the relationship with Kristy that the losses for Samantha would be lessened. I think the romantic ideal was that we would all be like one big happy family, without understanding the grief that birth mothers have to go through. We made assumptions that Kristy would be able to manage her grief and all of the other feelings related to the adoption, by knowing her own boundaries. Mostly, she *did* manage it quite well for many years, but then she disclosed information that we had all decided would be kept confidential until later in Samantha's life. I think Samantha is still dealing with the after effects of that disclosure, and that is painful for all of us.

We said this was an open adoption, but we were creating a charade of openness as long as we kept this secret. I would advise birth and adoptive parents to tell the truth, even if it is painful.

— Amy, an adoptive mother

Adoptive parents have got to understand that you are inviting someone into your life when you don't really know who they are. We had this intimate bond that we expected to be lifelong, but we had no control over that disclosure. Openness is really about creating an extremely intimate relationship with a stranger. Adoptive parents need to know how to manage that fact.

Samantha, Speaking at Age 17

My birth mother and I talked a few times a year, but it wasn't until I was about 13 that I considered meeting her. Once when my parents weren't home, Kristy called and mentioned the name Brandon. I said, "Who's Brandon?" and she said, "Your brother." I didn't get it at first. I thought that maybe he was in a different family; because I knew she had only one other son who was born after me. I asked if I could talk with him and she said no, because he didn't know about me. Finally I got it. The shock was so big that it turned my world upside down! I felt an incredible sense of betrayal, and I was outraged with both of my parents. I was also really sad because it felt like an important connection had been denied to me. I couldn't believe that other people in my life had the power to make decisions that kept my brother and me apart from each other for over 13 years. I felt like they were all living a lie at my expense. How could they have withheld that from me?

As soon as we could, Brandon and I were e-mailing, then instant messaging, then phone calls. After 2 years of talking, my birth mother wanted to know if we would fly to Florida to surprise Brandon for his 16th birthday, and we said YES! I felt so anxious and excited about meeting them, I was ready to pull my hair out on the plane! When I first saw my birth mother, I just stared, because it was like looking into a mirror. Then Brandon arrived and he knew exactly who I was. We had a great visit, but it was really hard for me to leave. Leaving has always been painful for me, but this time, it was like torture. I felt like I was being ripped apart. Some part of me wanted to stay and live with my brother and my birth mother.

Through all of this, my mother always knew the right things to say, and didn't take it personally. I wouldn't change my parents for anything, but I wish I had been told the truth from the beginning. It was not a big deal that I was adopted because I never doubted how much I was loved, but every adopted person should have the chance to have love from both families. I have never thought for a minute that my adoptive family is not where I am supposed to be. My younger sister in my adoptive family is my sister. Growing up together is what made us siblings—blood has nothing to do with it. Sure we are going to be different, but overall, I think relationships trump biology every time.

Kristy, Birth Mother of Samantha

I was 22 when I found out I was pregnant, and I was in no position to be raising another child as a single parent with a 14-month-old. I met Amy and Tom for the first time 3 days after the birth, and I could see that I was giving the baby a good home. Phone and mail contact was sporadic for the first 7 years, and I had it in my mind that we would meet when Samantha was much older. My biggest fear was about my son finding out. I wanted to protect him because I thought that he would hate me for what I had done. We had such a strong bond—I was a single mom with him until he was 9 years old when my husband and I were married. I kept telling myself that I would do it *later* when he was more grown up. I was afraid that Brandon couldn't handle finding out that he had a sister. He was all I had, and I didn't want to risk losing that connection.

I didn't want to keep secrets from my husband-to-be, so I told him about Samantha. He felt that I was being crippled by the secret and he was right! I would get off the phone with Amy, and Brandon would ask me who I'd been talking to and I would lie. The more contact I had with Samantha, the worse I felt about not telling Brandon. And the more I didn't tell him, the harder it got to tell. I was also hiding the photos we were exchanging because the older Samantha got, the more she looked like me. One night when Brandon was 14, I slipped and mentioned his name when I was talking to Samantha on the phone, and all hell broke loose! As soon as he found out, he wanted to call Samantha. He also wanted to tell everyone he knew that he had a sister, but *I* wasn't ready to have everyone know. That was when he got angry. He had found out that he had a sister, but now *he* had to keep her secret.

We decided to surprise Brandon for his 16th birthday with a visit from Samantha and her family. When they arrived, I was totally shocked because Samantha looks so much like me. It was very healing for my Mom and Dad because they could finally put a face to this child that they had never seen. I was so focused on how the visit was going for my parents, for Brandon, and for my other son, that I didn't think much about how it was going for Samantha and me. The night before she left, I thought, this is going great. I have a clear getaway: no recriminations and no pressure. Just then Samantha came through the door crying hysterically and said, "Why did you give me away?" I took a deep breath and said, "Sam, you look around and see us living well, but that is not what my life would have been if I had kept you. It was my only choice.

It had nothing to do with not wanting you—I just couldn't handle being a single parent of two children."

I gave Amy and Tom the right to be Samantha's parents 19 years ago, and I never wanted to interfere with that. Samantha has had a difficult adolescence, and I did not want to hear things that she wasn't going to tell her Mom and Dad. Once she called me with information that I thought was risky, and I hung up and called her parents. She read that loud and clear. I tried to shed some light on what my own rebellious teens were like, but I didn't want to give her a free pass like "My birth mom did that so it's OK." I never wanted her to use adoption as a crutch or as an excuse. I try to walk a fine line between supporting Samantha, and also knowing that she has to face this stuff herself. She was born to me, and we are alike in so many ways, but she is not mine, and I am not her mother. My advice to birth mothers would be to remember that you have a great responsibility to the child: you carried this child, you gave birth, you made a choice to bring this child into the world, and it is your responsibility to keep the door open.

My advice to birth mothers would be to remember that you have a great responsibility to the child: you carried this child, you gave birth, you made a choice to bring this child into the world, and it is your responsibility to keep the door open.

— Kristy, birth mother of Samantha

Brandon, Brother of Samantha:

I was 14 when I found out that I had a sister, and I wanted to meet her immediately. I understood why my mother felt she had to do an adoption, but I didn't get why it had been kept hidden all of these years. Almost two years after they told me, I came home and saw several people in the living room. As soon as I looked at Samantha, I knew exactly who she was. I could see myself in her, and she also looked like my mom. We had a great few days where we got to know each other, and then she had to go back home.

Over the last few years, Samantha has had a lot of hard times. She went through a phase that she wanted to live with us and reached out to me, but I really didn't know what I could do to help. She knew that her parents loved her, but she also wanted to be part of our family too. It seemed like she had a lot of feelings about finding out about me when she was a teenager. Samantha wanted to be more involved in our life, as if that would take away her pain. Looking back, I felt pretty guilty about not being able to help her, but I don't think I understood what she was going through. I am more involved in her life now, but everything we do can't make up for the pain that has already happened. It is so important to tell kids from the beginning. If adoptive and birth parents wait until the teenage years it just hits too hard. I want to tell birth and adoptive parents *don't lie to your kids.*

What have been some of the effects of full disclosure during the teen years on both the adoptive and birth family? How can adoptive parents be helped to think through their feelings about their child having a full sibling living in the birth family? What steps could be taken by a birth parent or an adoptive parent to support a sibling relationship such as the one described above?

Closed and Open Adoption within the Same Family

Deborah and her partner Polly have three children: Eliza age 14, Lydia age 13, and Grace, age 10. Eliza's birth mother is involved in their lives, as are Eliza's birth grandparents. Grace and Lydia were adopted from China and have no knowledge of their birth families. Being a lesbian couple, Deborah and Polly have faced unique challenges on the road to parenting. They juggle the complexity of raising three children, one adoption being fully open and two closed, and all three being transracial adoptions (interview, 2005).

Deborah

When we started the adoption process in 1990, we went to an orientation of one of the agencies that included open adoption. I remember the look of panic on some of the heterosexual couples' faces as people were talking about having a birth mother or birth father in their lives. That was no big deal to us, because we already would be two moms, and we were used to having other people in our lives become extended family.

When my daughter's birth mother came into our lives, we were nervous because we thought an agency would not let us adopt. Celia

From left to right: Lydia, Polly, Eliza, Deborah, and Grace. Deborah and Polly are the parents of Eliza, Lydia, and Grace. Eliza was adopted domestically and Lydia and Grace were adopted from China.

(not her real name) was accepting of us as lesbian parents because we were receptive to having an ongoing relationship. She has always been very committed to Eliza, but not always able to follow through. When Eliza was little, we didn't tell her that Celia was coming until the last minute, because we did not know if she would actually show up. That has actually helped Eliza come to her own conclusions about why her birth mother was not able to raise her, and she now has a balanced view of what it would be like if she had stayed with her birth mother.

People usually don't talk about class in open adoption, but from what I have observed, most adoptive parents are middle or upper class, and many birth parents are working class or poor. Often when Celia had to cancel, it was because of mini-crises: "I couldn't get to the job interview because my car was broken." We bailed her out a few times in the early years, because we had the resources to help her. We were also aware that as lesbians, it would have been much more difficult to adopt if we had not found Celia. I know it is not a politically correct word in adoption, but we were *grateful,* and we wanted to help her get on her feet. The differences in class play out in other ways. Eliza is quite a talented kid, and her birth mother clearly has some of the same abilities. Celia has been choked up at times watching the opportunities we have been able to give Eliza that Celia never had herself as a child. We have been able to help Eliza flower in a way that she probably would not have done if she had stayed in her birth family. That is definitely one of the bittersweet parts of open adoption.

When we were about to consider a second child, we had to ask ourselves if we could handle another fully open adoption. We knew that what we had with Celia was unique, and that it would be a difficult and lengthy process to adopt domestically. China opened up, and like many people, we thought it would be easier to do an international adoption. In hindsight, international adoption is certainly no easier—it is just different. It has been really challenging to raise children who do not know their birth families. Neither of our children feels alone in her Asian identity because we live in the Twin Cities, which is very diverse, but it is a lot of work to keep their language and traditions alive.

We wondered about the challenges of having both open and closed adoptions in our family, but we thought it would be good for them to at least have the experience of knowing a birth parent. We went back to China for our third daughter because Lydia was the only one in our family who had no connections to her biological family. We felt that it would be helpful to have another child in the family who at least looked like her, and shared parts of her story. Even though Lydia and Grace are so different from each other, I think they get something from having another sibling from the same country.

I wish we could give our other two children what Eliza has: knowing her birth mother and her birth grandparents. It breaks my heart because our other daughters clearly long for the connection. My daughter Lydia was 5 years old when we were reading an adoption story, and the animal was looking for his "other" family. I said, "Like your other family in China." And she said, "What do you mean my other family?" I explained for the millionth time, but for some reason it clicked this time, and she immediately asked, "What was the matter? Didn't she like me?" At that moment I was so glad to have Celia in our back pocket. I could say, "Lydia, you know how much Celia loves Eliza, but she could not raise her." I saw the fear drain from Lydia's face and she could see that this was not about her. Having Celia in our lives has made birth parents more concrete and less of a fantasy for our other kids.

Another bittersweet feeling I have is knowing that Celia can look at us, and know that she made a good choice, but I am sure there are two other mothers somewhere in China who wish they could do the same. We know that Lydia was with her birth family until she was 5 months old. There must have been a clampdown in her neighborhood—something happened for the birth mother to relinquish her child after 5 months. I wish we could show her what kind of life her daughter has now.

Once we were able to adopt our children, I threw myself into adoption and started an organization called Rainbow Families, a regional organization that has national influence in advocacy and public policy for gay and lesbian families. I am trying to make a world that is more supportive of gay and lesbian parents because it is so hard for us to be parents. Gays and lesbians don't take parenting for granted, and we tend to be incredibly conscientious by reading the adoption literature and attending workshops. Because the options are limited and the road to parenting more circuitous, gays and lesbians often take on some of the more challenging adoption situations: multiple foster-adopt kids, kids with physical and mental disabilities, and older children. I am continually moved and inspired at what gay and lesbian families have to offer in terms of being such good parents and so committed to family building.

What are some of the effects on adopted children of living with a sibling with a different degree of openness or no openness at all? How might those differences best be addressed? What are some of the challenges of being a transracially adopted child in a family with children of different ethnicities? How might an adoptive parent explain to a child that she was relinquished

I wish we could give our other two children what Eliza has: knowing her birth mother and her birth grandparents. It breaks my heart because our other daughters clearly long for the connection.

— Deborah, adoptive mother of three

when she was 5 months old? How might a birth parent be helped when considering placing a child in a family where parents are a different race or sexual preference?

Open Adoption between Best Friends

Ann and Brandy had a 15-year history of being best friends before they decided to enter into an open adoption. Ann's son Robert was adopted at birth from Brandy, his birth mother. Their relationship has been enhanced by becoming birth and adoptive parent to Robert. Other birth and adoptive parents would need assistance as they carefully considered the challenging issues that might arise when adopting a close friend's baby (interview, 2003).

Ann

Brandy and I have known each other since college, and were friends long before the decision was made to place her birth son, Robert, with me and my husband. We have been roommates, have survived a house fire, were in each other's weddings, celebrated the birth of her son, Jack, and mourned the hardship of my infertility. Our close friendship was made even more special when Brandy became pregnant with Robert. At that time Brandy and her husband were breaking up, and Jack was just an infant. She knew that she could raise one child as a single, working parent, but not two. She remembered a dream she'd had about carrying a child for us, and called to ask if we wanted to be the baby's parents.

Living with an open adoption with my closest friend has never been difficult. We never felt the need to set guidelines because our relationship as birth mother and adoptive mother grew naturally from our friendship. When you begin to date someone, you don't spell out beforehand that you'll see each other on alternate Saturdays, and talk on the phone every evening for 20 minutes. You just begin the relationship, and it develops as it goes. It's the same with us. We visit when it works, talk when someone has something to say, and send letters and pictures when we have an occasion to do so.

The big winner in this situation is Robert, who is blessed with two families, a brother, and has more grandparents than he can count. Brandy and Robert have their own relationship, but that doesn't make me any less his mother. There is a special place for Brandy in my heart: we have a strong friendship with the added benefit that Brandy is the person who allowed me to become a mother.

Brandy

Still overwhelmed with being a new parent, I found out I was pregnant when my son Jack was 10 months old. My marriage was crumbling, and

Making Room in Our Hearts

From top to bottom: Brandy, Jack, Ann, and Robert. Jack and Robert are full biological siblings. Brandy is the mother of Jack and birth mother of Robert. Ann is the adoptive mother of Robert and best friends with Brandy.

I knew that my close friend Ann and her husband were trying to adopt. I never would have considered adoption, but I remembered a dream in which I had a baby and gave it to them. I had absolute trust that they would make a wonderful life for him. Ann and Jim came to stay with me after the birth, and I shepherded them through the first few days

Left to right: Ann and Brandy. Brandy is pregnant with Robert, who will be adopted by Ann.

Our children are full biological siblings, and when they see each other about twice a year, they are inseparable. I know that they will have a relationship as brothers for the rest of their lives, and we all want to support that.

— Brandy, a birth mother

of parenting. It was really hard when it was time for them to leave, but having them with me was the best way to help me heal because I could see how in tune they were to Robert's every need. Eight years later, I think of Robert as their son first, but there is no denying that he is also a part of me.

Robert looks totally like his brother Jack. Our children are full biological siblings, and when they see each other about twice a year, they are inseparable. I know that they will have a relationship as brothers for the rest of their lives, and we all want to support that. I am absolutely clear about the decision I made and have no regrets. I could not have been an adequate mother to Robert given the situation at the time he was conceived. I think that if a birth mother was wavering, or less than totally sure about her decision, placing a baby with a friend could be a disaster. Ann and I are closer than we have ever been. She loves Robert as her son, and I think a piece of her loves him even more because he is my son, too. That is what has made all the difference: this is an adoption among best friends who are now family.

CHAPTER 9

Making It Work

Many prospective adoptive parents think, "I would like to be able to do an open adoption, I can see where it would be good for the child, but it just seems too hard and too complicated." Open adoption *can* be hard sometimes, and it is often complicated, so what makes it work for so many families? In this chapter we will discuss the difference between structure and process in open adoption, discuss the tools that are most helpful in effective communication, setting good boundaries, and managing conflict, followed by a look at the responsibilities of birth and adoptive parents. Finally, we will hear from a birth mother, an adoptive mother, and the 21-year-old son. The son says, "Knowing who and where I am from solidifies things for me. I wouldn't want to imagine my life without an open adoption."

Different Strokes for Different Folks

The experts in open adoption agree that no one type of open arrangement is right for every family. Some birth and adoptive family members interviewed here had a difficult time in the beginning stages, but grew closer when the child was older and expressed the need for more contact. Some were thankful they had developed these relationships in early childhood, as that allowed the child to grow up knowing his birth family. Other families said that they were more adept at developing relationships and maintaining good boundaries because they had the advantage of geographical distance between them and the birth family. Some families found ways to maintain connections that worked around mentally unhealthy or substance abusing members of the birth family, while others did not. For most of the families, finding a balance of connection, separation, and collaboration was a back-and-forth process that took several years to co-create. Grotevant and McRoy (1998), put it this way: "Over time, adoptive kinship networks will develop different relationship solutions as they engage in the process of arriving at a workable zone of comfort" (page 199).

Many of the parents interviewed listed the following traits as helpful to them in their open relationships: honesty, flexibility, trustworthiness,

Over time, adoptive kinship networks will develop different relationship solutions as they engage in the process of arriving at a workable zone of comfort.

— Harold Grotevant and Ruth McRoy, adoption researchers

and being respectful and non-judgmental. These are attributes that most of us aspire to in our lives, but they are not always so easy to practice. Shari Levine, of Open Adoption and Family Services in Oregon, encourages participants in open adoption who are facing challenges to draw from their altruistic values and try to take the high road:

> Open adoption relationships deserve our best efforts. When our fears lead us toward feelings of jealousy or being judgmental, it is important to take a step back and consider the long-term effects of our actions. Do they reflect the values we hold dear? Are we proud of the choices we are making? Are we truly serving the ongoing needs of our child (interview, 2005)?

Upholding the belief that openness is in the child's best interest can help families weather the ebbs and flows of open relationships, and even some of the storms.

Process versus Structure in Open Adoption

Each family in an open adoption has a unique way of handling it, which results in varying degrees of contact, intimacy, and sharing between the families. One adoptive family might see their child's birth mother up to three times per year, but for lunch visits that don't allow for much connection between the birth parent and the child. Another family, due to geographical distance, might only see the birth family once per year, but they make it an extended visit that includes the possibility of deeper relationships forming. In addition to having ample time with the birth parent, the child might be able to form connections between themselves and the birth grandparents, siblings, and other extended members of the birth family. It is not merely the type of contact, or the amount of time spent, that makes an open adoption open.

David Brodzinsky, coauthor with Schecter and Marantz of *Being Adopted: The Lifelong Search for Self,* offers valuable thoughts about the difference between the *structure* and *process* of open adoption. "Open adoption should never be confused with 'openness' in adoption. Openness is a process and goes well beyond the specific family structure of whether birth and adoptive parents make a certain number of contacts per year. Openness is a process that demonstrates a willingness to engage with each other, to be open to the possibilities presented by the relationship. It is a communicative process, not just a sharing of information, but a sharing of emotional openness" (2004).

"Genuine openness includes sharing adoption related emotions both within families and between families." The most important question Brodzinsky asks us is: "From the perspective of the child, which is more important? Family structure or family process?" His answer is emphatic:

Openness is a process that demonstrates a willingness to engage with each other, to be open to the possibilities presented by the relationship. It is a communicative process, not just a sharing of information, but also a sharing of emotional openness.

— David Brodzinsky, psychologist

Making Room in Our Hearts

Family process is *always* more important than structure. The quality of communication plays a much more important role in the success of relationships than the type or frequency of contact. What is more powerful in predicting the success of any familial arrangement is the kind of communication that exists: open, honest, non-defensive dialogue, not only about adoption but about any issue (2004).

The following story points out the importance of paying close attention to the process of these relationships even more than the structure.

Sara and Jay had a lengthy relationship with the birth mother of their daughter, who was now 20 years old. The adoptive parents felt strongly about maintaining an open relationship, and had visits several times a year with the birth mother, who lived only 30 minutes away. In addition, the daughter had been supported in spending time alone with her birth mother since her early teens. This family looked for all practical purposes like a fully open adoption, both in the structure of visits, regular phone calls, and the quality of communication, until I had the opportunity to interview the birth mother.

The birth mother had a very different experience of the quality of openness. Although she was glad that they had stayed in touch through her daughter's life, she didn't feel like she "had the place" to ask for more contact with her. "There were so many times throughout her childhood when she had school events, or when she performed, that I would have so loved to have seen her, and shared in her family's celebration. But they never asked me or suggested it and I always took my lead from them." She didn't feel that she could ask for a relationship that included being more involved in her birth daughter's life because "I didn't think it was my right and I didn't want to appear ungrateful."

This difference between the experience of the adoptive parents and the birth mother points out several issues. Sara and Jay began their open adoption in the mid-1980s, when birth parents were not encouraged to speak about their own needs and preferences. In the past, openness was often seen as a privilege for the birth parent, and one that could be revoked if she made a wrong move. This particular birth mother's position of relative powerlessness, and not feeling entitled to speak about her own needs, led to the adoptive parents' making all of the decisions about contact, without even knowing that they were doing so. When asked, the adoptive mother said that the birth mother was probably as satisfied about the quality of their relationships as she was. The structure was there, but the permission to communicate openly and honestly was lacking.

Clarifying Expectations

Although the quality of the communication is of the highest importance, the commitment to ongoing contact is also important if one wants to help a child develop an ongoing relationship with his or her birth family. One of the important steps adoptive and birth parents can take is to share their ideas about the kind of relationship they hope to develop, and their vision of what their relationships might look like 5 or 10 years down the road. Sometimes adoptive parents want a baby as quickly as possible, and they are afraid that they might lose a match by having complex discussions with the birth family about the future. However, having these discussions will clarify whether making a match would involve endless conflicts, or whether each party's vision is close enough that the two families could collaborate. One birth father felt that it was adequate to visit his birth son's family once every two years because that is how often he saw his own father, while the adoptive parents could not imagine anything less than annual visits. After discussing what kind of relationship they each wanted to build, they were able to collaborate on the frequency of visits. Carol Demuth, an adoption counselor and educator in domestic adoption at Buckner Adoption and Maternity Services in Texas agrees: "The vision-matching process can make the difference between those who become more of an extended family, and those who develop a pen-pal relationship."

Adela Jones, the director of domestic adoptions at Buckner, has developed tools for supporting open relationships. One of these is a "relationship profile" filled out by potential birth and adoptive parents that solicits their vision of the kind of relationship they want:

> We ask clients to think about what they value, and what values they want their children to have. We also ask them to think about the family traditions that impact on their lives: the kinds of food they eat or how they celebrate holidays. Is one family the kind that invites people to stop by when they are in the neighborhood, or are they the kind of family that puts things on the calendar and needs to be prepared? We also ask them to look at more profound issues like how loss is handled. Loss is a huge part of adoption, and we need to identify how each set of parents might deal with it so they could recognize how it plays out in the relationship (interview, 2005).

The clarification of expectations during the matching process is crucial to avoid the kinds of problems such as this one offered by Adela Jones:

> During the first meeting with prospective adoptive parents in July, the birth mother was assured that she would be considered part of the extended family. She asked if she could visit at Christmas and the couple answered "of course." In early December, the birth mother

One of the important steps adoptive and birth parents can take is to share their ideas about the kind of relationship they hope to develop, and their vision of what their relationships might look like 5 or 10 years down the road.

Making Room in Our Hearts

called to tell them her flight schedule indicating that she would arrive on Christmas Eve. The meaning of "extended family" for her was getting together for the holidays, on the holiday. Unfortunately, that is not the meaning it had for the adoptive parents.

This example points out how important it is to not make assumptions about the needs, expectations, or hopes of the other person, but to be sure that such issues are fully discussed ahead of time.

These vision-matching discussions can help birth and adoptive parents consider the reasons that they chose open adoption in the first place. Adela Jones reminds us that these relationships are more about values than about the number of visits per year. "Adoptive parents always ask us: 'What are your requirements for visits? How many times a year do I *have* to see them?' We try not to reduce an open adoption relationship to x number of visits or x number of phone calls. We ask people to look at it from a different point of view: What has experience taught you about how frequently a child needs to see or talk to someone in order to have a meaningful relationship?" This question focuses on the opportunities to be given *to the child* to develop a relationship with his or her birth family.

More Effective Communication

After almost 25 years in the field, Carol Demuth, who educates and counsels birth and adoptive parents, has found that many people need help in learning how to communicate difficult feelings in constructive ways. She attributes much of her understanding of better communication to the book *Difficult Conversations: How to Discuss What Matters Most:*

> Communication is usually occurring on three levels, but we hardly ever get to the third level of communication. The first level is what happened, the second is the feelings, and the third is the meaning of what happened. When people are upset, the feelings usually get spewed out all over the place without identifying what those feelings are. The conversation that is most often lost is what is called the identity conversation: what meaning did this event have for you? For example: "When she came over to our house, she walked past us, straight to the baby like we were not even there." The important issue is getting to the *meaning* of what happened, and then the adoptive family can identify that: "We felt discounted as people. That visit didn't feel like it was about us—it was about the baby." After recognizing the meaning of what happened, people are more able to be able to figure out how to talk about the problem (interview, 2005).

Difficult emotions like envy, resentment, and anger, often get in the way of constructive communication and can lead to conflict. When either party

We try not to reduce an open adoption relationship to x number of visits or x number of phone calls. We ask people to look at it from a different point of view: What has experience taught you about how frequently a child needs to see or talk to someone in order to have a meaningful relationship?

— Adela Jones, Director of Domestic Adoption, Buckner Adoption and Maternity Services finds themselves in a situation where seeds of discontent are coming up, its time to consider: why do I feel this way? Is this an echo of something that happened in my past? What are my needs in this situation, and how can I address them? Carol Demuth continues:

> One of the factors that most determines how these relationships develop has to do with how each side processes and communicates about their losses. If the birth mother is envious of what the adoptive mother has, and is not able to talk about it, it will get in the way. Adoption is asking two women to come together in a very intimate relationship, and *each one has what the other one desperately desires.* The adoptive mother wants to have given birth to the child, and the birth mother wants to have been able to parent. If they are able to communicate about their losses openly, then they can move on from there.

Setting and Maintaining Boundaries

The ability to set and maintain boundaries is one of the most important ingredients of a healthy open adoption. Adoptive parents often fear birth parents will want too much contact, and birth parents fear that adoptive parents won't follow through on their agreements. They each need to be able to voice their concerns, and set up arrangements that make it less likely that their respective fears will be triggered. The most important thing about boundaries is to talk about them from the beginning, and the second most important thing is that it is *never* too late to talk about them! Adela Jones reminds us, "Adoption is all about loss, and the accompanying intense emotions tend to obliterate good boundaries. If adoptive parents feel guilty, or take too much responsibility for the birth parent's grief, they may hesitate or be reluctant to set healthy boundaries. Birth parents, not clear about where the boundaries are, often cross them without even knowing that it is happening." Birth and adoptive parents need to remind themselves that they are embarking on new territory. It is understandable that they will need extra support as they try to clarify their needs and figure out how to make boundaries that work.

Boundaries need to be set by the adults, but as the child gets older, it is important for the parents to communicate with him or her about what they are doing and why. After a difficult visit with a birth mother who shared inappropriate details about her past with her 8-year-old birth daughter, the adoptive parents decided that the boundaries during the visits needed to be changed. She and her husband decided that the visits would not include alone time for the child and birth mother until they had assurance that the birth mother was able to be more careful about the information that she shared. It was important they talked openly with their daughter about why they were making the decision. They made it clear to the birth mother that they still wanted her in their life, but they needed to protect their daughter. Instead of coming to the conclusion that the birth mother was "bad" and couldn't be trusted, they made a boundary that protected them, and talked to the birth mother about what behavior would be needed in order to remedy the situation.

When Rhonda, the birth mother of a 5-year-old, had her second child, it triggered unresolved grief from the placement of her first child. Her sadness, combined with the demands of being a new parent, made it difficult to maintain a relationship with the adoptive family. Instead of separating and feeling bad about it, she explained why she needed to pull away. The adoptive parents understood, and requested that in addition to them talking to their son about the temporary separation, they wanted him to hear it from his birth mother, and she agreed. Not only did this help the entire adoptive family, it helped Rhonda realize that the door wasn't going to close because she needed some emotional distance. The act of sharing her painful feelings and coming to an agreement with the adoptive parents actually helped her in her grieving process.

Carol Demuth gives an example of the benefit of establishing boundaries early in the relationships. "We had a 6-year-old girl who told the birth mother that she wanted to call her Mommy. The birth mother understood why the child wanted to do that, but said that she didn't feel comfortable about it, and wanted to talk to the child's adoptive mother about it." In this case, the adults had established boundaries when the child was young, so the birth mother knew to have a conversation about this before making a decision on her own. When we say both birth and adoptive parents need to set and maintain boundaries, we do not mean that birth parents have an equal role in determining what is right for the adoptive family. This is not shared parenting!

One adoptive couple presented the following question about setting boundaries. When their daughter's birth mother was going to be married, she requested that the adopted child be in the wedding as the flower girl. The adoptive parents wanted to say yes to the birth mother as this was her first request of them, and it was such an important milestone for her. The adoptive parents knew that walking down an aisle unescorted would be painfully awkward for their shy 4-year-old daughter, but they felt worried about "doing the right thing." Wanting to please the birth parents may prevent adoptive parents from making decisions that they would make in any other situation. When I asked this couple what they would do if a close friend made the same request, it was as though a light bulb went off. They needed to do what they thought was best for their child, and that was to

When we say both birth and adoptive parents need to set and maintain boundaries, we do not mean that birth parents have an equal role in determining what is right for the adoptive family. This is not shared parenting!

not have her walk down the aisle, even though this was such an important event to the birth mother.

Another adoptive mom named Patty remarked: "The hardest part for me is that our birth mother cannot keep a job, so she is always feeling sorry for herself. When she comes for a visit, I spend a lot of time trying to give her ideas on how to keep moving forward. She doesn't have a support system other than us, so sometimes I feel like we have adopted two kids. It's exhausting at times!" It often feels risky to tell people what we need, but accumulated resentment doesn't bode well for any relationship. This adoptive mom could set better boundaries for herself by gently telling the birth mother how she is feeling, giving the birth mother some resources, and then trying to let go of her role as a career counselor.

For birth parents, their grief may make it difficult to set clear boundaries about their own needs. It may be difficult to share painful feelings with the adoptive family for fear they would interpret it as lack of commitment or regret. Wendy, a birth mother, found the first year after to be difficult because she never knew how much emotional space she would need from the adoptive parents. When the adoptive family called every other month as they had agreed, they sometimes found her depressed. Wendy felt terrible about the degree of sadness she was experiencing, and began to think that open adoption might not be for her. She was eventually able to say to the adoptive parents, "You cannot expect me to be normal right now. I do not know when I will be normal, and it has to be OK that I am the way I am." Talking honestly about the problem helped them make a simple change. They decided together that Wendy would be in touch when she could, unless it was over four months and then the adoptive parents could call. By acknowledging her grief while they discussed the problem of contact, Wendy was able to feel more accepted and willing to continue the relationship.

Adoptive parents are naturally more worried about being able to make boundaries with birth parents that have substance abuse or mental health problems. Don and Shirley struggled with these issues with the birth mother of their daughter. Shirley recalls, "It soon became evident that this would be a challenging relationship. Megan, the birth mother, was very demanding. We couldn't trust her decision-making ability, and found her to be very manipulative." Don recalls, "Even at the hospital, Megan told the nurses that we were buying her a car, and giving her a lot of money, none of which was true. So we knew from the beginning that this wasn't going to be easy."

Shirley remembers her conflicting feelings:

It was like having a teenage daughter, but I felt like I owed her something because my daughter was the most wonderful thing in the world. If we were going to have the relationship that we had agreed

Making Room in Our Hearts

upon, we thought we needed to do whatever we could to make it work. Looking back, I can see that I was bending over backwards because I felt like I owed her so much. It was as though I was trying to repay her for this gift. I now know that I don't "owe" her and could never repay her—adoption isn't about repayment (interview, 2003).

Shirley remembers what led her to making firmer boundaries:

One visit, Megan made inappropriate comments that scared our daughter. We could only guess what had been said, but our daughter was afraid that her birth mother would make her come and live with her. We knew right away that we needed to stop visits for a while. It was hard setting such tight boundaries, but we knew what we had to do, not only for our daughter's sake, but because we needed to not feel so intruded upon by her behavior.

Melina and Roszia remind us that boundaries can help us get to the benefits of openness, while maintaining healthy connections between birth and adoptive families:

Open adoption does not require that you live without rules or by someone else's set of rules. It is not an arrangement where the front door of the adoptive parent's home is always unlocked to the birth family. The difference between open and confidential adoption is that there are boundaries where there used to be walls. Walls, like the old Berlin Wall, are impenetrable. Boundaries, like border crossings, allow decisions to be made about when they can be crossed. Walls are put up by fearful people, willing to sacrifice some possible good to be sure that all the bad will be kept put (page 21).

Brenda Romanchik reminds adoptive parents to not feel guilty about making clear boundaries:

You need to make boundaries as though this person was not a birth or an adoptive parent; as though they were another relative or friend. Would you loan money to a friend who you felt was using it for drugs? *No!* Be honest about what you would do. You need to try to take out the extra emotional burden about being birth or adoptive parents, and make boundaries by deciding what is best for your family and for your children (interview, 2004).

This next story illustrates what can happen when an adoptive parent is unclear about setting boundaries, and the impact that can have on the child and the adoptive mom. Nanette is an adoptive mom who always felt a little guilty about "having another woman's child." Watching the emotional pain of the birth mother made her feel as though she were somehow to

> *Open adoption does not require that you live without rules or by someone else's set of rules. It is not an arrangement where the front door of the adoptive parent's home is always unlocked to the birth family.*
>
> — Lois Melina and Sharon Kaplan Roszia

blame. Even though her daughter was almost 13 years old, Nanette did not feel fully entitled in her parenting role, and she often bent over backwards to accommodate the birth mother. This led to a build-up of resentment and reluctance about maintaining the relationship with the birth mother. Thus, the daughter was left alone in managing her relationship with her birth mother, which only increased the daughter's anger toward her mother. This led to hurt and angry feelings on everyone's part, and caused Nanette to question the value of open adoption for her family.

The problems between the birth and adoptive family could too easily be dismissed as problems related to openness, when in fact, healthy communication patterns had never been established. The adoptive mother, 13 years after the adoption, was still walking on emotional eggshells in regard to the birth mother. Stretching beyond her limits, and not being able to set boundaries, Nanette grew angry with her daughter for whom she was "doing the open adoption." She was unclear about her role as the parent, which led her to withdraw from her daughter at a vulnerable developmental stage. If Nanette had examined her own feelings toward the birth mother, she might have been able to recognize the need to set boundaries. Doing an open adoption, allegedly for the child, was a disaster for the whole family.

This discussion about making good boundaries might sound as though intense feelings and complex emotions should always be handled with mature rationality. We know that it is not always possible to do that, and we should not always expect it in open adoption. When communication is difficult and adoptive and birth parents are not sure why they are reacting so strongly, they can seek out professional support and guidance.

Managing Conflicts

As in all families, we have to make a choice when conflict emerges. Do we let resentments, anger, or guilt permanently scar the relationship, or do we try to work it out? Adoptive parents need to remember that they are trying to build relationships that may last a lifetime. Shari Levine of Open Adoption and Family Services says, "All of the parties need to show a willingness to struggle with conflict without closing the door. By facing and resolving the difficult times together, we are demonstrating to the other party that our commitment to the relationship is heartfelt and lifelong. Weathering the challenges in relationships is what builds the essential ingredients of trust and respect."

Much of the conflict in open relationships evolves around differences about contact and is a natural and expected part of the evolving relationship. Melina and Roszia remind us to be particularly watchful about these issues:

You may feel threatened, betrayed, vulnerable, or out of control if it appears the level of openness you want is not satisfactory. If the adoptive parents withdraw from the birth parents during the first year, or seem to begrudge the birth parents the contact they had promised, it feeds the birth parents' fears that the adoptive parents will renege on their agreements. Resist the temptation to jump to the conclusion that you cannot trust each other. Reevaluating the agreement is a natural part of the process (page 164).

This is important advice to families at any stage of the process, but especially in the first few years when the adoptive and birth parents don't have a strong track record with each other. Beth, a birth mother to 5-year-old Jacob, underlines the importance of getting professional help in the early stages when trust is still being established. She remembers some rocky times as she navigated the beginning stages of her relationship with Jacob's parents.

The relationship with his parents consumed me during the first six months of his life because we had become so close during the pregnancy. It was especially hard for my family, which didn't really understand what open adoption meant. Although my sister accepted that the adoptive parents were the parents, she felt like I should be able to see the baby any time I wanted. Both my Mom and sister were dealing with their own feelings about relinquishing their rights as a grandmother and an aunt. None of us were prepared for the intensity of the feelings that arose, and that made it harder for me. I felt like I had to juggle their needs and mine.

When Jacob was 6 months old, Beth made plans for extensive travel abroad. As the trip approached, she grew increasingly concerned about the ability of her own family members to visit the adoptive family in her absence. Because she had felt strongly about contact between her immediate family and the adoptive family, she had been careful to include visits in her written open adoption agreement. But since placing Jacob, Beth had seen very little movement by the adoptive parents toward this part of their agreement.

"This was a difficult time for me and the adoptive parents, because we were still trying to figure out what our roles were. I started to feel like I was fighting to establish my role in their life and began to feel resentful. For the first time, I was afraid that they might not honor their agreements about contact." After a flurry of e-mails back and forth, Beth and the adoptive parents decided to ask for mediation from their adoption agency. They wanted to reach a shared understanding about the frequency of contact and come to an agreement about visitation with Beth and her family. A mediation/counseling session helped everyone clarify issues and recommit

You may feel threatened, betrayed, vulnerable, or out of control if it appears the level of openness you want is not satisfactory. Resist the temptation to jump to the conclusion that you cannot trust each other. Reevaluating the agreement is a natural part of the process.

— Lois Melina and Sharon Roszia

to the agreements. It gave each party the opportunity to feel heard by the other, recognizing that they had very different needs during this time, but still wanted to maintain openness.

Beth's advice to birth and adoptive parents would be to get counseling or mediation during the first year, especially when there are other members of the birth family involved:

> The mediation made a lot of difference because I was starting to feel like I had no power. Since the mediation, the adoptive mom has become very comfortable in *her* role, and that has helped me to feel more comfortable in *my* role. Recently, the adoptive family decided to move over 3000 miles away, where I will not be able to see them as often. We had five months to process that decision, and although it was hard for me, I have come to accept it. If we hadn't had counseling, I don't think we could have weathered the moving decision so well.

Reevaluation of agreements and roles may be an ongoing process well into the adoptee's teen years and beyond. Often conflicts emerge when things are not following an expected path. One adoptive mom recalled that she hoped to be a "best friend" kind of mom to her daughter during her teen years, but her daughter's intense conection with her birth family got in the way. Instead of getting angry with the birth mother, the adoptive mom put some limits on how high the phone bill could be. She also talked to the birth mother about disclosing worrisome information if the daughter was at risk in any way, and she decided to spend more time alone with her daughter. In this case, managing the potential conflict took the form of setting better boundaries, and recognizing the adoptive mother's own needs in this situation.

There are often differences in the ability of birth and adoptive families to maintain these relationships, and Adela Jones of Buckner helps put this in perspective:

> Some birth parents have a hard time staying in regular contact. When a disconnect happens, it is understandable that adoptive parents might feel reluctant to open up the door again as they do not want to risk the child being hurt or disappointed. This is an opportunity to help the child see why his birth parents were not able to raise him or her. When parents try to protect a child from the birth parents' difficulties, the child is robbed of an opportunity to better understand why the birth parents made the decision they did. Parents need to ask themselves whether their child is going to be more negatively impacted by the erratic connection to a birth mother, or whether the parents' decision to deny contact altogether would be more detrimental. Is there a middle ground such as establishing contact with birth grandparents who are

The mediation made a lot of difference because I was starting to feel like I had no power. Since the mediation, the adoptive mom has become very comfortable in her *role, and that has helped me to feel more comfortable in* my *role.*

— Beth,
a birth mother

more reliable or other extended family that can meet the child's needs (interview, 2005)?

Conflict is particularly difficult to handle once it has reached the boiling point and erupted in bursts of anger and resentment. This is what occurred when one adoptive mother, Nicole, felt as though she didn't want to do anything to offend the birth parent, and was therefore unable to adequately protect herself or her family. She accommodated to whatever situation the birth mother presented to her, even when she knew it was not healthy. On a few occasions, the birth mother sounded intoxicated on the phone, and the adoptive mother tried to ignore it, giving the message that this was OK. When the birth mother showed up intoxicated for a visit, the adoptive mom blew up in anger. Only then did she realize that she was not doing her daughter any favors by ignoring the problems her birth mother was having. Nicole remembers, "I felt so grateful for my daughter that I forgot I was the parent and was in charge of protecting her and our whole family from alcoholic behavior."

There are some adoptive and birth parents whose relationships are clouded with conflicts and the inability to manage them. Looking back, it is often easy to see the red flags that were present from the beginning of these relationships. In that kind of situation, a separation may be helpful in order for the adoptive and birth parents to regain perspective, institute more appropriate limits, and find better ways to communicate. Professional counseling or mediation may be helpful, especially by someone with experience in open adoption. Counseling sessions can help with finding possible solutions or resolving difficult feelings even if only one of the parties is willing to attend.

Birth and Adoptive Parent Responsibilities

Birth and adoptive parents need to acknowledge each other's role in helping the child develop a cohesive sense of self. In order to do that, they need to recognize what their responsibilities are to each other. Carol Demuth of Buckner reminds us, "The birth parents are working on grief over the loss of this child, and the adoptive parents are working on feeling entitled to be the parents of that child. We ask them right from the beginning: What are you going to do to help the birth parents deal with their grief? And what are you going to do to help the adoptive parents feel entitled to parent this child?"

Brenda Romanchik, a birth mother and adoption educator, thinks that we need to go further in educating birth parents about their responsibilities:

> Very few in the adoption field talk enough about birth parent responsibility. There comes a point where the child's needs are primary and you should be there for them. Birth parents shouldn't say, "Oh well,

this is more than I bargained for." Most birth parents will tell you that the first few years of visits *are* outside of their comfort level, but they do it because it is the right thing to do, and that should be the same for adoptive parents. It isn't a matter of comfort. Many agencies give the "comfort spiel" to everyone involved, but they are talking about the comfort of the adults and *not about the children*. I have seen too many kids who are hurt by birth parents who do not come through for them. Historically, adoption practices have worked to make birth parents feel dispensable, so we need to counter that by letting birth parents know the vital role they can play, and their responsibility to keep up the connection (interview, 2004).

Advice for Birth Parents

In her booklet "Being a Birth Parent: Finding Our Place," Brenda Romanchik lists several principles summarized here that will help birth parents create healthy relationships:

1. Try your best to not make promises you cannot keep: broken promises are destructive. Barring emergencies, birth parents should try to do what they say they are going to do.
2. Support the adoptive parents and the decisions they make. Remember that acknowledging the adoptive parent's right to parent will enable you to grieve your loss.
3. Respect the adoptive family's customs. With time and familiarity, you will learn what is acceptable and what is not.
4. Remember holidays, birthdays, and special days celebrated by the adoptive family. Learning about traditions is an important part of respecting who the adoptive family is, and who your child will become.
5. As the birth parent, be there when it is important. Being asked to school plays and special family occasions is not only a privilege it is an opportunity for birth parents to let their child and his or her adoptive family know that you value them.
6. Everyone has different temperaments, tastes, and abilities. It is important to acknowledge and accept these differences.
7. The birth parent needs to be flexible. It is important to remember that open adoption is done for the children. As children get older, they are going to have more to say about what they want out of the relationship. Be open to change, as everyone's needs shift over the years.

Very few in the adoption field talk enough about birth parent responsibility. There comes a point where the child's needs are primary and you should be there for them.

— Brenda Romanchik, adoption educator and advocate

Making Room in Our Hearts

Pointers for Adoptive Parents

Author of *The Spirit of Open Adoption,* James Gritter has a list of pointers for adoptive parents, some of which are paraphrased here:

1. Create an atmosphere of inclusion and belonging.
2. Let the relationship be reciprocal and balanced. Let the birth parents teach you.
3. Take the initiative to keep the relationship lively and current. Resolve to make the relationship work by holding up your end and more.
4. Communicate frequently. Keep cards, letters, and lots of pictures coming! Inform birth parents of significant matters.
5. Communicate clearly. When you don't know what is going on, ask! Don't presume too much. Double check to be sure you are clear about what the birth parents mean if you are ever in doubt.
6. Respect the birth parents. Honor their need to control their own lives, and their need for privacy. Take a genuine interest in them, but don't impose your ideas about how they should live.

Forgiveness

Forgiveness often sounds like a religious or spiritual concept; something that you have or you don't, not something that you could learn. Since the mid-1980s there has been actual research on the practice of forgiveness and its impact on improving relationships, enhancing self-esteem, and assisting in managing conflicts. At Buckner Adoption and Maternity Services, Carol Demuth has been using forgiveness as a tool to assist birth and adoptive parents, especially when conflict arises:

> A lot of people have a skewed view of forgiveness saying, "I am not going to forgive them because they don't deserve it." People don't have to *deserve* forgiveness. You can forgive someone even when what that person did was wrong, even when he or she is not sorry. You can forgive someone and there can still be consequences. The biggest misconception about forgiveness is that you do it for the other person. Actually, you forgive someone for your own benefit. Forgiveness frees up so much psychological and spiritual energy in your own life (interview, 2005).

We all know the experience of ruminating about a perceived or actual injustice inflicted on us by another person, and we are familiar with the cost to our well being of that kind of obsession. Many of the families that seemed particularly adept at dealing with the complexity of open adoption, spoke about letting go of the small issues, and trying to keep perspective

The biggest misconception about forgiveness is that you do it for the other person. Actually, you forgive someone for your own benefit. Forgiveness frees up so much psychological and spiritual energy in your own life.

— Carol Demuth, adoption counselor and educator

about who the other person is, and what her life experience has been. A critical component of forgiveness is the ability to picture yourself in the other person's shoes. Carol Demuth reminds us, "It is a matter of being able to see each other's vulnerability, to see that anger often masks fears. The very thing that you are angry at in this person is just a small part of who they are. Forgiveness requires work, determination, and practice, but it can transform the whole relationship."

An important area where forgiveness can be essential is between birth parents and their own extended family. Some birth grandparents made it clear that they would not support their son or daughter if they chose to raise the baby themselves. Brenda Romanchik shares a story of a birth mother who wrote to her about her experience:

> My parents were not supportive of my raising my daughter, and in fact, they did everything they could to prevent me. But now the adoptive family treats them as extended family members. My mother disowned me when I was pregnant, and said this child would not be her grand-child if I kept it, but *now* she gets to be a wonderful grandma like none of that happened. But I, who wanted this child, am never going to be a mom to her. It's not fair. I lost so much and she lost nothing.

This family as a whole, and not the birth mother alone, needs to find a way to acknowledge the pain of the past, but move forward with forgiveness. Brenda tells us that: "Forgiveness is an important part of the healing process. Whether this was the first time your family let you down, or just another in a long string of disappointments, forgiving them is the first step in accepting them as the imperfect human beings they are."

What makes openness work is for birth and adoptive parents to keep the reasons they are doing an open adoption front and center, and knowing that it is a process, not something fixed and rigid that they have to sign on to. Open adoption is definitely not "one size fits all," as each set of parents will develop unique relationships based on their personalities and needs. The issues that will surface in an open adoption are similar to those that most families grapple with at one time or another. Openness will make these issues more complex at times, but the solutions lie in the same arena as they do for all families: making and keeping good boundaries, improving communication, acquiring conflict resolution skills, and throwing in a little forgiveness to smooth the road ahead.

James Gritter summarizes his down-to-earth approach to helping open adoption work: "Be good to each other. Don't leave the other guy out there dangling. Give each other pointers, not directives. If you are puzzled, ask. Communicate with dazzling clarity. Anticipate misunderstandings—they are a fact of life in all relationships—and iron them out promptly. Forgive

From left to right: Patricia, Diane, Seth, and Richard. Patricia and Richard are the adoptive parents of Seth. Diane is his birth mother.

imperfections generously" (2004). These are wise words for all of us to try to live by.

Smooth Sailing: Good Boundaries and Clear Rules

Next we hear from the adoptive mother and birth mother of Seth, who, at 21 years old, has known his birth mother for most of his life. This family was one of many who moved in the direction of openness long before there was much support in the adoption community. They had the assistance of a facilitator who helped guide and support them as they took steps toward developing an increasingly open relationship. This family, like many others, has not had many complicated issues to deal with, and its road to co-creating an open relationship has been relatively smooth. Seth is now a young man in college, and his story reminds us of the positive effects of open adoption on the development of a strong sense of self (interview, 2003).

Pat, Adoptive Mother of Two

My son Seth's birth mother, Diane, was 14 when she discovered that she was pregnant, and chose my husband and me partly because she wanted her child to be raised in a multiethnic family. Diane was adopted herself, her adoptive mother is Japanese, and her adoptive father is white. I am Japanese American and my husband is Jewish, and Diane later told us that she was drawn to us because of this similarity to her own parents.

A few weeks after the birth when Seth was placed with us, we met Diane and her parents for the first time. We only knew each other's first names and the general area where we each lived, and had no idea that we would ever see each other again. It was important to me that Diane be given a record of her son's life, so we agreed to send pictures and letters every 3 months for the first year, exchanged through our social workers. At the end that year, Diane asked if she could continue writing to us, but she didn't want us to feel obligated. On the contrary, I felt so close to her that I definitely wanted to continue to correspond. Our social worker remarked that she had never seen a relationship quite like ours, and suggested we think about opening it up.

Diane's response to our question about opening the adoption came in the form of a wonderful audiotape of her and her parents expressing their interest. This was completely novel at the time, but we had the advantage of working with Ellen Roseman, an adoption facilitator who has been a strong advocate for openness for over 25 years. Ellen was instrumental in encouraging us to keep our options open in terms of developing a relationship with Diane. My husband and I felt that having an ongoing connection to our children's birth mothers would be important to both the children's sense of identity, as well as to the emotional well-being of their birth mothers.

Slowly but surely, we took additional steps toward more openness with Diane and her parents. When Seth was around 4, we had a chance to meet Diane's mother when she was in town visiting friends. It was a very special evening for all of us. Later, after the big earthquake in our area, Diane's mother called to see if we were okay. This began a series of phone conversations between Diane and me. When Seth was almost 5, we asked if Diane wanted to talk with him on the phone. I knew this would mean a lot to her, and I wanted Seth to be able to have this connection. A few months before Seth's 5th birthday, I thought that it would be good to share the celebration with Diane and her parents, so we had our first visit since Seth was placed with us. The following year, on his 6th birthday, we invited them to stay with us at our home, and we have continued this annual gathering for many years.

Soon Diane and her boyfriend were coming to see Seth on special occasions like school performances. When Diane announced she was getting married, Seth was adamant, "I want to be the ring boy in your wedding," and so he was. We have both felt honored to be able to participate in this stage of Diane's life, as well as later when she received her Master's degree. After years of having our support and encouragement, Seth has developed his own unique relationship with his birth mother. I couldn't have engineered this—it evolved organically whenever it felt

> *After years of having our support and encouragement, Seth has developed his own unique relationship with his birth mother. I couldn't have engineered this—it evolved organically whenever it felt right.*
>
> — Pat, an adoptive mother

right. We were extremely fortunate to have formed a strong relationship with a woman who has always been very respectful of our role as Seth's parents, as well as warm and loving to both Seth and us.

We all consider Diane, her husband, and her parents an important and special part of our family. Looking back over the past two decades, I can honestly say that Diane and her family have become as much a part of our family as anyone. I am probably closer to her than I am to some members of my own family. Seth has gone through many changes as he separates from us, and builds a life of his own, but the openness we have created between our families has not changed, it has only deepened.

Diane, Seth's Birth Mother

I never intended to have an open adoption, but it would have been very difficult to let go and not know how he was doing, so we agreed to exchange letters for the first year. That was very healing for me, but I was also a little afraid of getting attached in a motherly kind of way. I knew that I didn't want that, and I was a little hesitant when Pat suggested a visit to celebrate Seth's fifth birthday. I was extremely nervous about that first visit because I didn't know what to expect. The visit was great, but when I was leaving, it all hit me. I broke down and started to cry, because the reality of it finally got to me. You have life growing inside you for 9 months and then it is suddenly gone. I had to find a little compartment to put these feelings. *Openness takes all those feelings out of the compartment.* It was hard in the beginning, but I think in the long run, the benefits of staying in touch are so much greater than the pain of leaving. I didn't know that then, but I know it now. He is almost 21 years old!

When he was about 9, I realized that we were establishing a relationship that would last forever. We are alike in so many ways: how we look, how we express ourselves, our passion about life. My relationship is definitely not a mom—more like a big sister. Dick [adoptive father] and Pat have helped me become more comfortable with the birth mother role, and they have kept me involved and made me feel welcome. What has made all the difference is good boundaries. I cherish the fact that I have always been able to put some boundaries around my contact with Seth and his family. I was never there to step on any toes or change the rules, and I think Pat and Dick always knew that. So we all had really clear roles from the beginning: I am definitely not his mom, I am his birth mother.

> *It was hard in the beginning, but I think in the long run, the benefits of staying in touch are so much greater than the pain of leaving.*
>
> — Diane,
> a birth mother

Seth, Speaking at Age 19

Adoption makes sense to me because I have contact with my birth mother—she is a real person. I know why she made that decision when she was 15 years old—she cared about me then, and she cares about me now. If I wasn't able to talk about the adoption with her, I am not sure the choices she made would feel as valid to me. As I get older, I can see that every stage had me asking different questions, and each question that was answered filled one of those little holes. You never know if someone is telling you the truth until that person looks you right in the eye and says, "This was my mistake, but you are better off for my decision." This person wasn't just giving me up because she had made a mistake and didn't want to think about the consequences. She really had an interest in me then, and she still does. Since I was about age 14, our relationship has become much deeper—it's kind of like having a good friend or an older sister.

I have always felt that my parents just get it. They never seemed to feel threatened by my relationship because they have understood how important it is to me. Diane and I totally look alike—I see myself in her in a lot of ways. We are both passionate, and even have some of the same kinds of rebelliousness, but my relationship with my birth mother has never been a wedge between my parents and me. We have had some of the usual teenage stuff with me wanting to be a separate individual, but it has never come down to the question of which person I was born to. That would seem like a low blow to go there—to compare my parents to Diane in any way.

Even though Diane and I are really close, I have never thought of her as a parent, because basically she is not. My parents are totally different people with very different roles. For someone to be a parent, there needs to be an underlying agreement that this person is in charge. These parents are the parents I have always had, and I don't know why I would go and switch over to my birth mother for parenting. People's fears about that seem kind of irrational to me. Now that I have separated some from my parents and am away at college, my relationship with Diane has not changed. Because I am more independent, it doesn't mean that she has a different role in regard to my decisions.

Recently, I was talking to a girl at school who didn't seem very happy and was having a hard time. The more we talked, the more it became clear that she had a lot of stuff she was pinning on the fact that she was adopted. She had absolutely no connection to anyone in her birth family, and seemed to have a thousand questions about who she was. She seemed even more confused than most kids in college. She had no idea about what steps to take next, and blamed a lot of that on having been adopted. I was able to explain to her that I didn't have those same kinds of questions, even though I was also adopted. The fact that I have known my birth mother all these years has made such a difference in

From left to right: Diane and Seth. Diane is Seth's birth mother.

my life. I know who I am and where I am from. It has helped solidify life for me.

When a birth mother gives up a child, it's a sacrifice for the benefit of the child. Open adoption is not about sharing a child. I am both people's child, but my birth mother is not my mother. My adoptive parents will always be the only parents I know. I would tell people considering open adoption that it is important to get around your personal fears. If you love this child, you can do so much more for them by filling in those holes that burn inside of their minds. In so many ways, that is just what a child needs from their parents.

Open adoption is not about sharing a child. I am both people's child, but my birth mother is not my mother. My adoptive parents will always be the only parents I know.

— Seth,
an adoptee

CHAPTER 10

A Call for Change

The numbers of birth and adoptive families that embrace some degree of openness in adoption are growing each year, and will continue to transform the landscape of adoption, both in the United States and around the world. Whether these families are prepared to face the complexities of these relationships depends in large part on how adoption professionals see their role in preparing and educating all parties, before and after the adoption takes place. This chapter will examine the role of adoption professionals in preparing the way for healthier open relationships, and discuss some of the best practices of open adoption. We will also look at some of the ways that openness is expressing itself in international adoptions. Finally, the profiled family features a 26-year-old woman who has spent her entire childhood and young adulthood in an open relationship with her birth mother.

Child-Centered Adoption Education

Many of the experts who have led the way in promoting increased openness agree that it is incumbent upon adoption professionals to provide education that includes the possibility of children knowing their birth families. Where openness leads in the future is dependent in great part upon whether adoption professionals take up the call to provide child-centered education and support to *all* birth and adoptive parents. Families will falter unnecessarily if they have not been prepared for the inevitable challenges that open adoption brings. When hitting the first major communication difficulty, some will turn their backs on these arrangements, assuming open adoption is not for them.

Currently, open adoption support and education varies greatly across the country, even among advocates of openness (Grotevant and McRoy, 1998). Some agencies are known for their child-centered approach, and foster relationship building between adoptive and birth parents from the beginning of the process. Others support the concept of openness, but do little other than facilitate meetings between the birth and adoptive parents, and let them take it from there. Many other professionals fall somewhere in between: recognizing some of the benefits of openness and providing education during the adoption process, but rarely inviting the participants to look at the challenges of these relationships over time. The majority of those interviewed here reported that very few of their adoption service providers fostered discussion between the birth and adoptive parents about their ideas and hopes of how the relationship might evolve in the future.

Expectant parents sometimes receive education of the highest caliber that looks at the possible benefits to the child, but they are more likely to get the basic version that goes something like this: "You get to choose who will raise your child and hear how they are doing from time to time." Brenda Romanchik, director of Insight, Open Adoption Resources and Support, fields calls from birth parents around the country, and verifies that this is more of the norm than the exception:

> Most of the calls I get tell me that birth parents have no idea that open adoption could include visits. Agencies are telling them that they can get letters and pictures once a year, and "isn't that wonderful." These are people in crisis and they often feel that anything they get is more than what they deserve, so it is doubly important that they be fully informed about all of their options (interview, 2004).

Since there are currently no nationally recognized standards for educating clients about openness, every agency, attorney, or adoption facilitator can do as much or as little as they choose in terms of pre- and post-adoption education. In many cases, adoptive parents are often given a brief talk that goes something like this: "You will be able to meet the birth parents and you will be able to get medical information straight from them. Then you can decide if you want to develop a relationship if it feels comfortable for you." This laissez-faire approach makes openness seem like one option among many on an adoption buffet table where you get to choose whatever makes you comfortable. Openness *is* something that adoptive parents need to *choose*—it is not mandated, nor should it be. However, we know enough about the negative impact of not knowing one's birth parents, and the positive effects of having open relationships, that it behooves adoption professionals to support openness as a basic standard of adoption practice.

The lack of ethical guidelines and standards is especially true of the Internet where birth and adoptive parents can relate directly to each other, without any education or preparation about forming relationships. They may be represented by attorneys or facilitators who have had little or no training in child welfare ethical practices or openness in adoption. Some might look at the independent ways that birth and adoptive parents meet on the Internet as an important freedom in that they no longer need an intermediary to find each other, and merely use an attorney or agency to

Most of the calls I get tell me that birth parents have no idea that open adoption could include visits. Agencies are telling them that they can get letters and pictures once a year, and "isn't that wonderful."

— Brenda Romanchik, adoption educator and advocate

complete the necessary legal arrangements. Unregulated and unrestricted access to getting whatever you want in terms of adoption has been successfully touted as a new freedom. However, relinquishing children is a child welfare issue, and as such, requires adequate education about what are life-altering decisions for everyone, but especially for the child. As in many other arenas, current laws and regulations have not caught up with the rapidly altered social practices that technology has made possible.

In Chapter 7, we heard from Josephia, a birth mother who said that "I didn't feel like it was my place," to ask for more contact with the adoptive family. One can hear echoes of the subservience expected of any marginalized group in the way she spoke about herself. Far too often, people who have decided that they were unable to parent, make the painful decision to locate a family to raise that child, only to find themselves relegated to a position of relative powerlessness after the adoption. This is not merely a surviving remnant of the history of secrecy and shame in closed adoption, it speaks to the current reality that many adoptions still take place without frank and supportive discussions by adoption professionals that value the potential role of birth parents in a child's life. If we are to help bring birth parents out of the realm of fantasy and conjured-up images, we need to give them authentic models of the positive role they could play in the child's life. All birth parents, at every stage of the adoption process, need education and support to understand the positive contribution they can make to the child's developing sense of self.

Other experts note with dismay that some agencies, attorneys, and facilitators offer openness more as a carrot to entice birth parents than as a genuine commitment to ethical standards. Carol Demuth at Buckner Adoption and Maternity Services states that:

> Many agencies have gone into openness as a marketing tool so that they can attract more birth parents. We recommend that birth and adoptive parents ask providers what they mean by open adoption. If clients do not fully understand *why* they are choosing openness, the problems that arise can seem insurmountable. If I could wave a magic wand, I don't think there should be adoption outside of agencies that provide the appropriate child-centered education (interview, 2005).

Increasing numbers of adoption professionals understand that it is not enough to let birth and adoptive families meet, and then be on their own to negotiate these complex relationships. Some agencies are some are setting the bar about what constitutes the "best practices" in open adoption. Shari Levine is the executive director of Open Adoption and Family Services in Oregon, one of the oldest agencies in the country that specializes in open adoption. The agency was co founded in 1985 by Jeanne Etter, a

All birth parents, at every stage of the adoption process, need education and support to understand the positive contribution they can make to the child's developing sense of self.

pioneer who understood that if open adoptions were to succeed, there needed to be education about the benefits to all members of the adoption triad. Understanding the benefits for the birth and adoptive parents can often make the difference between a pretense at openness and genuine relationship building. Shari Levine has observed:

> When openness is not held as an intrinsic value by an adoption agency, adoptive parents tend to approach it reluctantly. They often view openness as a *concession* to the birth parents, not as a philosophical foundation that will benefit all parties. We have fully embraced open adoption *not as a choice, but as a standard of the best in adoption practice.* To assist adoptive parents and birth parents to explore and address their fears, we provide free-of-charge ongoing counseling. We believe that relationship building is the cornerstone of a successful open adoption, so we provide the education and guidance necessary for adoptive parents and birth parents to create healthy, lifelong relationships that meet the ongoing needs of the child (interview, 2004).

The Role of Counseling

Most experts agree that counseling is an important component of the open adoption process, and that models of intervention geared to these families need to be developed. David Brodzinsky reminds us that:

> Openness is fluid. We cannot assume that what happens at the time of placement will be the same down the line, but we have not yet developed programs for these families as they negotiate these complex relationships over time. An arrangement is made and often that agency is out of your life. What happens when that arrangement isn't working or when boundary issues emerge? (2004)

Adoption professionals often discuss the first year or two after placement, but we need to be available to families through all of the developmental stages of the child's life. Many of the interviewed families said that they would have liked additional assistance in the first few years of defining these relationships, especially to hear from others who were attempting to keep family ties. Others said they needed support when they reached a milestone: when either the adoptive or birth family had additional children, married, or divorced. Several spoke about the need for more support in terms of how to incorporate sibling relationships into their family. The teen years found several youth and their parents struggling about independence and separation as well as the role of birth parents during this tumultuous time.

The interventions that some of these families found useful were usually one to three sessions of counseling or mediation that helped

When openness is not held as an intrinsic value by an adoption agency, adoptive parents tend to approach it reluctantly. They often view openness as a concession *to the birth parents, not as a philosophical foundation that will benefit all parties.*

— Shari Levine,
Director of Open
Adoption and
Family Services

them talk about difficult feelings, clarify roles, and assist with boundary making. Most of these problems were not mental health issues, per se. They were simply working out arrangements for which there are few models, and they needed help from professionals who knew how to support the unique dynamics of open adoption.

However, finding counselors who understand the dynamics at play in open adoption may not be so easy. An otherwise fine therapist, who does not appreciate the complexity of managing these relationships, might make suggestions that are not appropriate. That is why it is best that agencies see themselves as providing ongoing support for these families as they develop their relationships on an as-needed basis. Financial resources are an issue, but a portion of the money that adoptive families pay could go into a pool for future counseling needs, in addition to families being offered low-fee or sliding-scale services. Creative solutions could be found, but only if the agency shared a vision of being a child-centered organization whose purpose was not solely to find babies for adoptive parents, but to support birth and adoptive family members as they seek to build a relationship that works for each of them.

Including Birth Fathers

It is obvious from the lack of birth father representation among the profiled families included here, that they were minimally involved in these particular open adoptions. When they were involved, it was difficult for them to speak about their experience. Several birth fathers who were interviewed reported residual shame and unresolved feelings about having been relegated to second-class status in the adoption process. Brenda Romanchik has some ideas about how and why this occurs:

> Agencies frequently cater to the birth mother's negative emotional reactions to the birth father. When the birth father is placed out of the picture as a partner in making this child, he becomes someone to be dealt with for legal purposes only. Too often we look at the birth mother as the primary birth parent, and let her decisions be the ones that guide the adoption. Adoption professionals need to design programs that fully acknowledge that the birth father is equally involved in the co-creation of a child (interview, 2004).

Shari Levine of Open Adoption and Family Services states that they have done over 900 adoptions, and they could count the numbers of birth fathers involved on one hand. That led them to engage in a project to find out more about birth fathers.

Too often we look at the birth mother as the primary birth parent, and let her decisions be the ones that guide the adoption. Adoption professionals need to design programs that fully acknowledge that the birth father is equally involved in the co-creation of a child.

— Brenda Romanchik, adoption educator and advocate

We found that they had different needs that weren't being addressed. First, they want to know what role they will have in the adoption process, and they need the steps spelled out very clearly. Men are doers—they need to know how they can help. We can start by helping them be involved in choosing the adoptive parents. They also need to see themselves represented in agency brochures and outreach, just as the birth mothers are. We recognized that we needed to educate the adoptive parents about explicitly welcoming the birth fathers into the open adoption, and discussed ways to do that (interview, 2005).

One birth father that was interviewed remembers this all too typical experience with adoption. "I remember when I went to the agency to sign the relinquishment papers. No one asked *me* how I was feeling, or if I had been informed about all of the options. No one ever asked *me* if I thought I could raise this child. No counseling was offered. No nothing. We have to remember that even though a woman carried the baby, that child is part of both a man and a woman." It is no accident that while birth fathers are not adequately represented here and elsewhere in adoption practice, adoptive fathers are frequently not as actively involved in maintaining open adoptions as are the adoptive mothers. The job of maintaining communication with birth families often includes details such as deciding which photos to send, starting the family holiday letter to the extended birth family, choosing the gift to send when a birth parent marries, and many other details. The concrete and emotional work of maintaining and developing open relationships all too frequently become tasks that are mostly done by the adoptive mothers and birth mothers.

The reasons for this gender imbalance are beyond the scope of this book, but suffice it to say that adoption is an equal opportunity for women *and* men to fully participate in family building. Adoption professionals need to listen to birth fathers *and* adoptive fathers to hear what they need in order to be more included in the process. An initial welcoming connection between the adoptive father and the birth father may be the one that invites the birth father into the open relationship. This will support the full inclusion of men, invite both men and women to share the logistical and emotional responsibilities of open adoption.

Where Do We Go From Here?

Speaking as an advocate for higher ethical standards in adoption, Brenda Romanchik is in the unique position of having heard from hundreds of birth family members about their experience with the adoption system. "We should start by acknowledging that birth parents have a responsibility to consider parenting, and the adoption system has an ethical obligation to help them do that. The whole philosophy of the child welfare system is aimed at strengthening families, and trying to get them back on track through reunification services. But far too often, when a woman comes to an adoption agency, she is not given the opportunity to even *discuss* keeping the baby. That should be the first question: "Have you thought about what you might need in order to raise this child yourself?"

Molly, the birth mother in Chapter 4, spoke for many when she said, "No one, at any point, ever mentioned to me the possibility that I could keep this child and how I might do that. It's not that I was ready to parent, but no one even gave me the right to consider that possibility." Adoption professionals need to begin by making certain that the decision to relinquish a child is made only after a thorough exploration of whether the birth mother could raise the child, and that the birth parent understands some of the long-term ramifications of relinquishment for herself and for the child.

The adoption decision should also be made without the immediate economic circumstances of one's life being the sole or primary deciding factor. Many birth parents find themselves in precarious economic circumstances that greatly contribute to their decisions regarding adoption. However, there are many who if given the right financial assistance, could look beyond their current crisis to a time when they might be more equipped to handle the responsibilities of parenting this particular child. Birth parents should be supported in considering all of their options by someone that is not invested in having them relinquish their child.

Kathleen Cleary is the executive director of the Consortium for Children in Northern California, which offers training on the use of mediation for permanency planning in the public adoption system. She agrees that changes need to be made:

> We have a two-tier system for adoption. Child welfare law covers one tier where we offer family reunification, services, and support, and it has to be done through an agency. In "independent adoption" we have another group of children that have been adopted, but in many instances, there is little oversight of these adoptions. People go on the Internet, talk to a facilitator who may have no qualifications, and receive inadequate education and counseling. These are two different standards and we need to make one child welfare system that puts the best interest of the child first (interview, 2004).

Although there is not agreement about whether adoption should be under one public system, it is clear that the increasingly commercialized approach by many who have not been trained in child welfare practice, makes it very unlikely that their clients are being given the tools to make thoroughly informed decisions about relinquishment or about openness. Brenda Romanchik agrees:

We should start by acknowledging that birth parents have a responsibility to consider parenting, and the adoption system has an ethical obligation to help them do that.

— Brenda Romanchik, adoption educator and advocate

Until adoption is regulated, it will be very hard to move toward what we know are best practices, but there are some steps we can take to move us in the right direction. Adoptive parents are often paying huge amounts of money to support women through their pregnancies. Too often, it can make women feel obligated to follow through on an adoption plan. If money were not so much a part of the equation, there would not be such an imbalance in these relationships. One solution might be that financial aid for birth parents could be drawn from a pool of money, not from a particular adoptive family, thus lessening the feelings of obligation toward placing with a particular family.

With this story, Romanchik continues with an example of how distorted parts of the adoption *business* have become:

A staff member of an adoption agency once said to me, "We have *our girls* come back three to four times because they are so satisfied with our services." I said, "You mean to tell me that women are placing three to four children with you, and you see that as a *success?*" Some of these women were becoming serial birth parents, and that was not being looked at as something that was extremely dysfunctional! It was seen as a *success* because it produced more babies. This agency was not addressing birth control, self-care, self-esteem, grief and loss, or the effects on the relinquished children. Serial birth mothers are a gravy train! Why would they want to stop women from having babies if they could place them?

The above anecdote may be one of the most egregious examples of the lack of ethical standards in adoption practice, but this agency did not exist in a vacuum. Many adoption agencies are in the *business* of adoption, and as a business, their clients are the adoptive parents. They frequently do not provide the counseling and benefits advocacy that might lessen the likelihood that a women would choose adoption, because to do so would lessen the children available for their clients. Even agencies that attempt to meet the needs of the birth parents in an ethical manner, may not always look carefully at their priorities.

I had the opportunity to consult with a young birth mother who had recently placed her second child for adoption in less than two years. She was an adoptee herself, but up until the time I saw her in therapy, no one had discussed the role her own adoptive status may have played in "looking for unconditional love by having babies, but babies that I was not in the position to keep." If the current and future emotional health of this birth mother had been considered of the utmost importance, she would have received counseling that addressed adoption loss, identity issues, self-esteem, and birth control and sexuality. If she had received this during the vulnerable time before and after the relinquishment of her *first* child, she may not have had to face the relinquishment of another child a mere 14 months later.

It is unlikely that the negative influences of money in an unregulated field such as adoption will be solved any time soon, but steps could be taken to identify the effects of looking at adoptive parents as the prime beneficiaries of adoption services. Asking several important questions would assist agencies and their staff as they attempt to become more child-centered: How might we change our services in order to better represent the needs of all of the parties in adoption? How might we help birth parents make a decision that is right for them, not only in the midst of the crisis of pregnancy, but five years down the road? What policies and procedures would we have in place if we wanted to assure that all parties understood the benefits and challenges of openness in adoption?

Recommendations for Child-Centered Open Adoption Services

1. Explore fully with each expectant parent, the possibility of her raising the child herself: discuss with the expectant parent how she might do that, what resources would be needed, and how to obtain them. These discussions should be followed by an adequate period of reflection on the birth mother's part, before she proceeds with the choice of adoption.

2. Pre- and post-adoption education for both birth and adoptive parents should include the effects of adoption on each stage of the child's life: early childhood, middle childhood, the teen years, and young adulthood.

3. Discuss the benefits of openness for birth and adoptive parents, and for the child. Facilitate discussion about expectations and hopes about future contact. Educate birth parents about the important role they can play in the child's life, and also educate adoptive parents about the birth parents' role in the child's life.

4. Educate both birth and adoptive parents about the life cycle of open adoption, identify challenging issues, and teach basic communication and conflict management skills

5. Provide counseling or mediation for these families for adoption-related issues throughout the life span of the child. Make these services widely available through sliding-scale fees.

6. Create specific program elements to empower birth fathers, and lessen their invisibility in the adoption process. Educate adoptive fathers about their role in maintaining openness and the possibility of keeping a connection with the birth father.

7. Make attempts to lessen the role that money has played in the placement of children. Consider other ways that low-income and impoverished birth parents could have their financial needs met instead of relying on potential adoptive parents to pay all maternity-related expenses.

8. Do not refer to agencies, attorneys, facilitators, or counselors that do not uphold minimal child welfare standards in their practice and whose interest is solely in the adoptive parents and the fees they will pay.

9. Educate the general public about openness, in order to create a more understanding and welcoming community. Respond to inaccurate media representations of open adoption.

10. Exert influence on local colleges and universities to train social workers in a child-centered approach to adoption. Encourage the development of curriculums that reflect the best practices of adoption.

Calls for Change Extend Beyond Borders

The desire for knowing more about one's self and one's origins is a transcultural and transnational phenomenon.

The gradual move toward more openness in domestic adoption has not only changed relationships between birth and adoptive families, it has highlighted the experience of adopted persons and their desire to know more of their own history. Just as in domestic adoption, many of the calls for change in international adoption are coming from adoptees themselves. Their desire to feel connected to all of who they are as human beings is part of the same human impulse that drives openness in domestic adoption.

Many adoptive parents turn to international adoption because they have an interest in a particular country and culture, and some see themselves as rescuing a child from the effects of institutionalization and poverty. In many countries, scant information about birth parents is available, with no opportunity to meet or exchange identities, and in some countries, birth parents are completely unknown. Some adoptive parents choose international adoption, in part, because they want to avoid having to deal with a relationship with birth parents in a domestic adoption, especially as more domestic birth parents desire some degree of openness.

Almost 200,000 children have been adopted from Korea since the mid-1950s, many being infants of mixed racial heritage as a result of the large American military presence during the Korean War and its aftermath. Many of the Korean adoptees have returned to their birth country as adults, looking for information and connections to their past, just as many in the most recent Chinese diaspora are likely to do the same in the future. The desire for knowing more about one's self and one's origins is a transcultural and transnational phenomenon.

The professional understanding that culture and ethnicity are important parts of an adopted person's identity and need to be honored, is a relatively recent phenomenon. Thousands of the adoptees from Korea were placed with families in the United States who had little understanding of the need to integrate the child's culture into their lives. The predominant view was one of assimilation—that the faster adoptees could become "American," the better. Susan Soon-keum Cox is the Vice President of Public Policy at Holt International, the adoption agency that pioneered the boom in foreign adoption that started in Korea. In an American Radio Works documentary entitled *Finding Home: Fifty years of International Adoption,* Cox states, "We were transplanting children from one country and culture to another, children of a different race and ethnicity—those were huge issues. It had never been done, particularly within the child welfare community."

Since the early 1980s, there has been a gradual erosion of this strict assimilation model, and taking its place is a multicultural model that seeks to integrate the children's culture into their new life with their adoptive family. More adoptive families are making it a priority to assist their children in developing their unique ethnic identity. We can see the effects of this changed attitude in hundreds of culture camps operating throughout the country, a multitude of workshops on transracial adoption, and special trips back to the country of origin to see the orphanage or locate a foster parent where the child lived before the adoption. Honoring the country of one's origin is part of a deeper understanding of the need for internationally adopted children to know more about who they are. One adoptive mother of a young girl from Viet Nam put it this way, "We will never have any access to my daughter's birth family. That door is closed for us, but we look at Vietnamese culture as her birth family, and we have integrated that into our home and family life."

Leceta Chisholm Guibault, the adoptive mother of Tristan, who was profiled in Chapter 5, allowed herself to be deeply affected by the voices of birth parents and adult adoptees, in addition to the often heard concerns of adoptive parents. In doing so, she has become a spokesperson for openness in international adoption, and understands the obstacles that exist:

> I personally know several adoptive parents of children from China who were glad they picked China because they would not have to deal with birth parents. One said, "When my child asks what I know about her birth family, I will honestly be able to say: nothing." These parents felt *comforted* by the fact that their children's birth parents were not in the picture, and there was no way that they would be in the future. But now that their daughters are 9 and 10 years old, those same parents are seeing them grieving, asking why, and wanting as much information as possible. Now they understand the difficulty of

Honoring the country of one's origin is part of a deeper understanding of the need for internationally adopted children to know more of who they are.

having absolutely no history or relationships with the birth family to share with their children (interview, 2005).

There is not a general movement toward openness in international adoption in terms of meeting and forming relationships between adoptive and birth parents. However, the greater appreciation of the need of adopted persons to know their true history, will slowly but surely, begin to erode the seemingly impenetrable doors of this historically closed system. All it takes is for a few families like Tristan's to search out pieces of information, to begin to pry that door open just a little. Once finding and connecting to a child's birth parents becomes a possibility, others will follow. There are a myriad of issues that would need to be addressed and carefully considered, not the least of which is the impact on the birth parents in their respective countries. But as we saw from listening to Tristan's birth mother, in spite of the fact that openness was completely foreign to her and others in her area who had relinquished children, she found the experience to be healing for herself and her remaining children.

Fully open adoption in the United States began with a few families at a time, until a critical mass began to affect the whole of adoption practice. Just as in domestic adoption, those who call for international change in this adoption are the adopted persons themselves. In an article in *Brain, Child*, Melanie Springer Mock notes:

> A good number of adult adoptees have critiqued the mythology of happily-ever-after, (in international adoption) noting the many negative aspects of foreign adoption: the big business that international adoption has become, the displacement caused by a child's move to a new culture, and the longing for one's past that never abates. And while memoirs by adoptive parents rarely focus on their child's biological parents, for adult adoptees, that initial loss—the separation from the mother who bore them—becomes an essential focus.

That "essential focus" will continue to inform and shape the experience of adopted persons and increase the desire for more openness in both domestic and international adoption.

Openness in Adoption—Another Form of Family Building

As a society, we have all been changed by the increasing fluidity of the structure of families. We have a wide body of knowledge about divorce, step and blended families, gay and lesbian families, and multiracial families. We now have a wide body of knowledge about openness in adoption, and pioneers in the field have been refining this knowledge since the early 1980s. What is needed now is a commitment from all adoption professionals that is similar to the one that is asked of these families: put the long-term interest of the children at the center of program decisions, and consider relationships between birth and adoptive families through the lens of the child's eyes.

In the professional adoption community there is one expression that is heard most frequently: adoption is a lifelong process, but to support this lifelong process means the commitment of services, resources, and vision. Encouraging open adoption before relinquishment, but not providing adequate post adoption services, often leaves families struggling in their own private ways. Adoption is not a private matter, even if a private attorney and a private facilitator arrange it. Adoption is, and always will be, a public institution that has great significance for children's welfare. Openness has transformed the institution of adoption, and will continue to do so well into the 21st century. Adoption practice needs to change in order to better serve the families that have made a commitment to each other for the sake of their children.

Two Generations of Openness

This is the first family interviewed for this book, and it is fitting that they are the last to share their story. They have been relating as an extended family for over 26 years (interview, 2003).

Colleen, Adoptive Mother of Dara

When we began our adoption process in 1978, contact between birth and adoptive parents was extremely rare. My sister told us about a young woman who was considering adoption, and we began having conversations with Tricia, an 18-year-old who lived in the same town where I grew up. Tricia felt uneasy about staying in the small town, and chose to spend the last few months of her pregnancy living with us. In 1967, I had placed my son for adoption and it was a horrible, secretive, and shameful experience, and I wasn't even allowed to *see* the baby. Years later, it didn't make sense to stop connecting with Tricia after the birth, so we stayed in contact through letters and photos.

When my daughter Dara was young, I attended support groups through PACER: Post Adoption Center for Education and Research, and listened to adult adoptees talk about growing up not knowing anyone from their birth families. I remember their angst about not knowing who they looked like. Many of them never let their adoptive parents know how they were feeling because they were afraid it would hurt them. I just knew that wasn't the kind of parent I wanted to be.

When Dara was 6, Tricia announced that she was getting married and asked us if Dara could be in the wedding. I remember thinking, "I can't see why not." There were 10 children in my family growing up, and one more was always better. My father welcomed everyone to

In the professional adoption community there is one expression that is heard most frequently: adoption is a lifelong process, but to support this lifelong process means the commitment of services, resources, and vision.

From left to right: Dara and Tricia. Tricia is Dara's birth mother.

our table, and I just knew that more love was never a bad thing. I love seeing Dara's personality in her birth mother and her birth mother in her. I like Tricia, and Dara has parts of *all* of us in her. Now that Dara has had a child, and I am a grandmother for the first time, that child is especially important to me, but she is also important to Tricia, who is her grandmother too. I don't need proof that my granddaughter "loves me the best." When she sees me, she puts her arms out to me and that is enough. I don't care if she also gets love from others—I actually welcome it. Really, is there ever too much love?

Dara, Speaking At Age 25

I remember being told that Tricia was the mom whose tummy I grew in and my mother was the mom who took care of me. My mom would say, "We are both mothers, but we are different kinds of mothers." I don't know how she did it, but she never felt threatened by having my birth mother in the picture. When I was 6, Tricia got married and I was the flower girl in her wedding. When I was 8, she had a boy who I consider

Making Room in Our Hearts

Dara, Cynthia, Jim, Christopher, and Colleen. Colleen and Jim are Dara's adoptive parents, and Cynthia and Christopher are Dara's children.

my brother, as I do her other two sons. I don't consider them my half brothers—I just call them my brothers. When I was 11, I began to fly to Wisconsin every summer to visit my mother's family and Tricia, and we always had a great time together.

I can't quite describe the relationship I have with my birth mother. It's sort of a cross between a big sister and an aunt and a mom, but not in the same way as my mom. But I think what it is, is like nothing else. She is closer than an aunt would be, and different from a big sister, but not quite a mom. She is my birth mother, not like any other relationship. It is hard to put a name to it. Sometimes, she is almost like a grandma, spoiling me. You have to keep in mind that she has three sons and I am the only girl, so we really enjoy doing girl stuff together. I have never felt rejected or cast away by my birth mother, because Tricia has always been a part of my life. It feels like she loved me then, and loves me now.

When I got married, Tricia and her family were invited. It wasn't an issue at the wedding because everyone knows the situation. The only surprise was that my birth grandmother, who had never been close to me, wanted to come to my wedding. She had a very hard time with the adoption, and had wanted Tricia to put that period of her life behind her. She felt it was scandalous that I was the flower girl at Tricia's wedding! It was like she was saying to Tricia, "You are finally becoming a respectable married woman, and you've got your illegitimate child going down the aisle with you!" But by the time that *I* got married, she had turned a corner, and was able to accept the relationship that Tricia and I had built over the years.

I feel completely rooted in my adoptive family. My birth mother and her family are extended family, not more and not less.

— Dara

A Call for Change

149

In June of 2002, my mom and dad were in Wisconsin visiting their family and Tricia's family, when they had a horrible car accident. My mother and others in her family were badly hurt, and my grandmother was killed. Tricia was so important to all of us through that whole time. They were all rushed off to the hospital, and Tricia became a center for communication and support. My sister and I stayed with Tricia as we dealt with this intense family emergency. This made us even closer—dealing with a serious accident together like any family would. My dad was really emotional and wrote Tricia a letter telling her how much it meant that she was part of our family, and had gone through this with us. He said it all in one expression: "She is not *like* family—she *is* family." I feel completely rooted in my adoptive family. My birth mother and her family are extended family, not more and not less.

Tricia, Dara's Birth Mother

I knew that I wasn't ready to be a parent at 18, but I also knew that I never wanted a child of mine to feel like I had rejected her. So when I heard about the possibility of placing my child with a family that was open to contact, I wanted to hear more. I had known someone who had placed her child through the closed system, and there was no way that I was going to go through the same kind of pain and secrecy that she went through. Never knowing if your child is alive or dead, doing well, or not. I knew I wanted something different.

Don't get me wrong—the first few years after the relinquishment were horrible. I was in almost unbearable pain. But slowly, the pain lessened, and I began to get a sense that I could get past it. I would remind myself that someday I would be able to have a relationship with this child. In the beginning, I had no idea about how this would go: what if they changed their minds? Colleen and Jim were always so reassuring, but I still didn't want to step on any toes, so it was easier to keep some distance those first few years. When she was about 4, I began to develop more of a relationship with Dara, who treated me like a combination of a favorite aunt and a fairy godmother.

Things began to change for me when I had my oldest of the three sons I have now. Fears kept cropping up throughout the pregnancy. I felt like I wasn't going to be able to keep this baby either—that someone was going to take it away from me. But parenting helped me heal like nothing else could. It didn't replace Dara, but it gave me the opportunity to parent, and that was very healing. I have always considered Dara to be a sister to my kids—I don't say half sister, I say sister. She started coming to visit every summer when she was 11, so my kids consider her part of our family. My second son seemed especially attuned, asking questions like: "Why doesn't she live with us? Is she still really sad about not living with you?" I would let him know that she had a wonderful family, and that was where she belonged. To this day, if I am in a market and someone asks how many kids I have, and I say three, my 11-year-old son will correct me publicly and remind me that I have four children, not three! So they look at it from their own vantage point.

This reminds me of one of the more challenging aspects. People look at open adoption as if it is weird. They are usually surprised and a little shocked, not necessarily negative, but they just do not know what to make of it. It is almost like telling them that you have a child that died—they just do not know what to say. I think professionals could do a lot more in spreading the word about open adoption and how it works. Looking back, I wish someone would have sat down with us and facilitated discussions about the kind of contact we would be having, and what our expectations and hopes were for the future.

I definitely have some advice for birth parents. I felt that the pain of separation would rip me apart for the rest of my life. I never thought the pain would end, but being involved in this way has been the only way I could have healed. I went to support groups for birth parents, and met many who had relinquished their children years before. No matter how long ago it was, whether it was five months, 5 years, or 15 years, it seemed like they were never able to heal.

However, I don't want to give the impression that there is not any ongoing pain in open adoption. When Dara had her own child, I felt like I had to process another level of loss. I had come to terms with the loss of parenting Dara, but now I had to face that this was my first grandchild and I could not be her "first grandmother." Yes, I am involved, but it is not the same. Open adoption is no panacea, but I think it is critical for the children. It is horrifying to me that they still practice completely closed adoptions in the United States. Kids need to have that connection.

As Dara has gotten older, things have changed. When she went to college, she stopped visiting as often, and I worried that she wouldn't be as connected now that she was on her own. Now things have settled into a new pattern, and I think we all feel good about it. Even my mother, who has treated this like a family scandal for 25 years, has come around. After years of wanting this to be kept secret, she could see that it has been good for Dara and good for me. Dara's wedding was a way of coming full circle. Dara was an adult, she was going to be leaving home and building her own family, and we were all there to celebrate and mark this passage—healing the circle in a way.

Looking back, I wish someone would have sat down with us and facilitated discussions about the kind of contact we would be having, and what our expectations and hopes were for the future.

— Tricia, birth mother of Dara

Closing Thoughts

Openness gives children the gift of possibilities, for now and for the future. It is not a cure-all, but it creates the possibility for a stronger sense of permanence and identity.

—Patricia Martinez Dorner

From the beginning of this book the terms *open adoption* and *openness* have been used interchangeably, when they actually mean different things. *Open adoption* is already a misnomer, as it was initially called *open* in opposition to the *closed* system of the past. The word *openness* does a much better job of describing the process of keeping family ties, as we have seen that these relationships require flexibility and emotionally honest communication in order to thrive. Openness is not only about the arrangements that are made between birth and adoptive families; it is about a fundamental shift in the entire landscape of adoption. In his book *Adoption Nation*, Adam Pertman states "… expanding openness is the central characteristic of the adoption revolution" (2000, page 17). Looking at openness from this broad perspective, we see that it encompasses other dimensions beyond the move away from the secrecy of the closed system. It includes a shift away from birth parents having to cut all ties, and toward a positive role for them in the life of their child. It includes a shift away from believing that a child starts his or her life with the adoptive parents as a blank slate, and toward an acknowledgment of the birth family's role in forming personality and temperament. The shift includes adoptive parents moving away from feeling threatened by birth parents, and toward feeling fully entitled to claim this child as their own, while knowing that a connection to birth parents can assist their child in developing a cohesive sense of self.

Many of the adoptive parents interviewed for this book wanted to convey their commitment to helping their children grow up feeling connected to birth families who were unable to raise them. It was that child-centered commitment that allowed many of these families to move away from their preconceived ideas of what constitutes family, to welcoming and embracing people who were initially strangers. Both birth and adoptive parents spoke about the beliefs and values that sustained them in the process, much more often than they spoke about "how-to-do" an open adoption. The essential beliefs that were often cited as touchstones for their relationships were these: that their children's sense of self would benefit by keeping family ties, that including birth family members would not lessen one's right to parent, and that having relationships with their birth parents would not confuse children.

If it were not for the fact that adoptive parents want so very much to parent, and that birth parents are not able to parent at a particular time, these people would rarely find themselves in each other's lives, but they do. And all differences aside, one person will parent the other person's child. Because of that connection, whether they are in each other's lives monthly, every few years, or not at all; whether they like each other or tolerate each other; whether they open their hearts with acceptance or not; they will be related to each other for the life of that child. There *are* ties that bind, and heredity is one of them. Even if birth and adoptive parents never meet, they will always have a connection through the life of that child. As I said in my story, "She is my daughter's mother—my daughter is her daughter. Her flesh is now of my flesh. Her creation is my joy. She will always be part of me, as you are part of her."

Most of the interviewed birth and adoptive family members recalled a time when they "got it"—when they truly understood why they were doing this, and what a difference it could make to their child's sense of self. Once that happened, they were not so troubled by the complexity of these relationships, and not as fearful of the uncharted terrain that they were traveling. Many of them understood that making these commitments would involve extending themselves, but they saw it as being no different from being parents who extend themselves to provide piano lessons for a musical child, get the right doctor for a child with a medical problem, or who cheer at soccer games for a child who is athletically inclined. It is the birthright of all children that those who raise them try to see them in their wholeness, with their strengths and weaknesses, and their unique special needs.

What we most need to remember is that *every* adopted child has unique special needs that go beyond the usual definition of learning or developmental problems. All adopted children were separated from their family of origin. Whether this separation occurred at birth with the adoptive parents standing by with open arms, or involuntarily through the child welfare system, or on the steps of a government building in China, that separation and its effects will shape the life of the child in ways that are both subtle and profound. Both adoptive and birth parents need to understand that no matter how much love and caring was involved in their decisions, no matter how carefully the separation was handled, that child will spend some part of his or her life trying to integrate that separation and loss into a cohesive sense of self. As birth or adoptive parents, and as professionals, we have an ethical and moral obligation to try to assist adopted children with that process of integration.

Recently, I was lying on the living room couch, with my daughter snuggled beside me, while we read together from a book called *A Dog's Life*. My daughter was reading, and she came to a part where a man threw two puppies out the window of his car onto a parking lot. Later, someone came by and saw the pair of puppy siblings, chose the one that looked best to take home with her, and left the other one shivering, scared, and alone on the pavement. As soon as the words were out, I knew that my daughter would have a reaction. I had barely finished the thought, when I turned to her and saw her taking in a lungful of air before she started to let out a loud anguished protest: "I hate this book," she suddenly screamed as she grabbed the book and threw it in the floor. Yelling now, with her full body reflecting her hurt and rage, "That's not fair! He shouldn't have done that. It's not fair that they can't be together—they are brother and sister. It's not right! He shouldn't have just picked one and left the other one alone. I hate him!! I hate this book!!" As her distress escalated, it became absolutely clear to me, from the intensity of her reaction and the depth of her pain, that this was much more than an 11-year-old angry at being exposed to the unfairness and cruelty of the world. I had seen this before. It was the tip of the iceberg rising up above the water, revealing some of the depth and breadth of what lies beneath. This was about adoption. This was about her birth mother having made the decision to relinquish her, then going on to have other children and choosing to raise them.

Would an open adoption have made these moments disappear? Not completely, but I believe it would have lessened the intensity of her reaction, and greatly reduced the depth of her sorrow. When my daughter's rage and hurt subsided, we talked once again about why her birth mother made the decision that she did: she was not able to parent *any* child at the time of my daughter's birth; she did not know my daughter, she did not know who she was or who she would become; she just knew that she was not ready to be a mother. Later in her life, when her situation had changed, she felt she was able to raise other children. Her father and I acknowledged our daughter's anger and sadness, and I believe she felt heard and understood. But if she had experienced a caring relationship with her birth mother for most of her life, I believe that she would have had a significantly different reaction to this story. Maybe we could have referred to a letter written by her birth mother explaining why she did what she did, or picked up the phone and called her, the birth father, or someone in her birth family. Most importantly, reading the story of rejection and abuse would not have tugged at her heart in the same way because she would have had direct experience that her birth mother cared about her now.

We know that openness should not be held up as a panacea for the losses inherent in adoption, but there are other considerations that should be made when weighing its benefits. Kathleen Cleary of the Consortium for Children in Northern California has said, "Lessening wounds is not a good enough reason to make a case for open adoption. The question is, do adopted children have the right to be whole? And if they do, that means they have the right to maintain connections, where appropriate, with their families of origin." Other voices from the adult adoptee community have gone further and said that to be able to connect to the people who gave you life is not only a question of ethical adoption practices, it is a question of upholding a basic human right to one's full identity.

Every child who joins a family through adoption has the right to be whole, but it is often difficult to separate the question of psychological and spiritual wounds from the right to be whole. That is precisely what emotional wounds are—they are fractures in our sense of wholeness, a rupture in our sense of being OK with ourselves and with the world. Birth and adoptive parents and adoption professionals must work together to lessen some of the psychological and spiritual challenges that come with adoption, at the same time as we work to support adopted children in their journey toward wholeness. Let us end by listening once again to the voices that matter most:

> **Danny:** I would be a completely different person if I had grown up without knowing who I was and where I came from. Open adoption has allowed me to be the person I was intended to be—with a connection to all of the people who made me what I am.

> **Juliana:** I know that if I had had the option of connecting to my birth family when I was younger, I wouldn't have felt so lost. Not knowing these things can build and build until you are lost inside. I feel so different as a person now that I know who I am.

> **Seth:** I would tell people considering open adoption that it is important to get around your personal fears. If you love this child, you can do so much more for him or her by filling in those holes that burn inside your child's mind. In so many ways, that is just what a child needs from his or her parents.

It is the reflections of those most impacted by adoption, the adoptees themselves, that can guide us, sustain us, and point the way toward keeping family ties through open adoption. May our hearts be open enough to hear them.

Lessening wounds is not a good enough reason to make a case for open adoption. The question is, do adopted children have the right to be whole? And if they do, that means they have the right to maintain connections, where appropriate, with their families of origin.

— Kathleen Cleary, Consortium for Children

Resources

General Adoption

Babb, L. A. (1999). *Ethics in American adoption*. Westport, CT: Bergin & Garvey.

Carp, E. W. (2000). *Family matters: Secrecy and disclosure in the history of adoption*. Cambridge, MA: Harvard University Press.

Franklin, L. (1998). *May the circle be unbroken*. New York: Harmony Books.

Ito, S., & Cervin, T. (Eds.). (1999). *A ghost at heart's edge: Stories and poems about adoption*. Berkeley, CA: North Atlantic Books.

Johnson, P. I. (1992). *Adopting after infertility* Indianpolis, IN: Perspectives Press.

Koening, M. A., & Berg, N. (2000). *Sacred connections*. Philadelphia: Running Press.

Melina, L. R.(1986). *Raising adopted children*. New York: Harper & Row,

Melina L. R. (1989). *Making sense of adoption*.New York: Harper & Row.

Pavao, J. M. (1998). *The family of adoption*. Boston: Beacon Press.

Pertman, A. (2000). *Adoption nation*. New York: Basic Books.

Rosenberg, E. B. (1992). *The adoption life cycle: The children and their families through the years*. New York: The Free Press.

Steinberg, G., & Hall, B. (2000). *Inside transracial adoption*. Indianapolis, IN: Perspectives Press.

Wadia-Ellis, S. (1995). *The adoption reader; Birthmothers, adoptive mothers and adopted daughters tell their stories*. Emeryville, CA: Seal Press.

Open Adoption

Dorner, P. M. (1997). *How to open an adoption*. Royal Oak, MI: R-Square Press.

Gritter, J. (1989). Adoption without fear. San Antonio, TX: Corona.

Gritter, J. (1997). *The spirit of open adoption*. Washington, D.C.: Child Welfare League of America.

Grotevant, H. D., & McRoy, R. G. (1998). *Openness in adoption: Exploring family connections*, Thousand Islands, CA: Sage.

Kaplan-Roszia, S. and Melina, L. (1993). *The open adoption experience*. New York: Harper Perennial.

Rillera, M. J., & Kaplan, S. (1985). *Cooperative adoption*. Westminster, CA: Triadoption.

Silber, K., & Dorner, P. M. (1989). *Children of open adoption*. San Antonio, TX: Corona.

Silber, K., & Speedlin, P. (1991). *Dear birthmother*. San Antonio, TX: Corona.

Understanding Adoptees

Brodzinsky, D. M., Schechter, M. D., & Henig, R. M. (1992). *Being adopted: The lifelong search for self*. New York: Doubleday.

Eldridge, S. (1999). *Twenty things adopted kids wished their adoptive parents knew*. New York: Dell.

Krementz, J. (1988). *How it feels to be adopted*. New York: Random House.

Lifton, B. J. (1994). *Journey of the adopted self: A quest for wholeness*. New York: Basic Books.

Van Gulden, H., & Bartels-Rabb, L. M. (1995). *Real parents, real children*. New York: Crossroad.

Watkins, M., & Fisher, S. (1993). *Talking with young children about adoption*. New Haven, CT: Yale University Press.

Understanding the Birth Parent Experience

Gritter, J. (2000) *Lifegivers: Framing the birthparent experience in open adoption*. Washington, DC: CWLA Press.

Jones, M. B. (1993). *Birthmothers, women who have relinquished babies for adoption tell their stories*. Chicago: Chicago Review Press.

Mason, M. M. (1995) *Out of the shadows: Birthfathers' stories*. (Howard, O.J. Publishing)

Romanchik, B. (1999). *Birthparent grief; Being a birthparent: finding our place; Your rights and responsibilities*. Royal Oak, MI: R-Squared Press.

Severson, R. (1991). Dear birthfather. Dallas, TX: House of Tomorrow Productions.

Shaefer, C. (1991). *The other mother:A woman's love for the child she gave up for adoption*. New York: Soho Press.

Grief and Loss

Jewett, C. (1982). *Helping children cope with separation and loss*. Boston: Harvard Common Press.

Roles, P. (1989). *Saying good-bye to a baby: Vol. I: The birthparent's guide to loss and grief in adoption*. Washington, D.C.: Child Welfare League of America.

Tatelbaum, J. (1984). *The courage to grieve: Creative living, recovery, and growth through grief*. New York: Harper & Row.

Communication

Fisher, R., & Brown, S. (1988). *Getting together: Building relationships as we negotiate*. Boston: Houghton Mifflin.

Smith, M. J. (1985). *When I say no, I feel guilty*. New York: Bantam Books.

Stone, D., Patton, B., & Heen, S. (1999). *Difficult conversations: How to discuss what matters most*. New York: Penguin Books.

Tannen, D. (1992). *That's not what I meant*. New York: Ballantine Books.

Adoption Organizations for Information, Advocacy, and Support

National Adoption Information Clearinghouse

Children's Bureau/ACYF, 1250 Maryland Avenue, SW, Eighth Floor, Washington, D.C. 20024

Telephone: (703) 352-3488 or 888-251-0075; Fax: (703) 385-3206; e-mail: naic@caliber.com

NAIC offers information on all aspects of adoption for professionals, policy makers, and the general public. The Clearinghouse develops and maintains a computerized database of books, journal articles, and other materials on adoption and related topics, conducts database searches, publishes materials on adoption, and gives referrals to related services and experts in the field. NAIC also maintains a database of experts knowledgeable in various areas of adoption practice.

North American Council on Adoptable Children (NACAC), 970 Raymond Avenue, Suite 106, St. Paul, MN 55114

Telephone: (651) 644-3036; Fax: (651) 644-9848; e-mail: info@nacac.org;

Website: http://www.nacac.org

Founded by adoptive parents, the North American Council on Adoptable Children is committed to meeting the needs of waiting children in the foster care system and the families who adopt them.

American Adoption Congress, PO Box 42730, Washington, D.C. 20015

Telephone: (800) 888-7970; Fax: (202) 483-3399; e-mail: ameradoptioncong@aol.com

Website: http://www.americanadoptioncongress.org

The American Adoption Congress (AAC) is an international network of individuals and organizations committed to honesty and openness in adoption and to reforms that protect those involved from abuse or exploitation. Membership is open to adoptees, birth parents, adoptive parents, professionals, and all others who share a commitment to the AAC's goals.

Evan B. Donaldson Adoption Institute, 525 Broadway, 6th Floor, New York, NY 10012

Telephone: (212) 925-4089; Fax: (775) 796-6592; e-mail: info@adoptioninstitute.org

Website: http://www.adoptioninstitute.org

The Adoption Institute seeks to improve the quality of information about adoption, to enhance the understanding and perceptions about adoption, and to advance adoption policy and practice.

National Adoption Center (NAC), 1500 Walnut Street, Suite 701, Philadelphia, PA 19102

Telephone: (215) 735-9988; Fax: (215) 735-9410; Toll-Free: 800-TO-ADOPT; e-mail: nac@adopt.org

Website: http://www.adopt.org

The National Adoption Center expands adoption opportunities for children throughout the United States, particularly children with special needs and from minority cultures. Through the Learning Center, adoptive parents and prospective adopters can take an online parenting course to expand and enrich their understanding of adoption. The course focuses on parenting skills, especially those needed to raise children with special needs.

Center For Family Connections, 350 Cambridge Street, Cambridge, MA 02141

Telephone: (617) 547-0909; Fax: (617) 497-5952

Website: http://www.kinnect.org

Serves individuals and families touched by adoption, foster care, kinship, and guardianship, as well as blended families. Offers education, consultation, advocacy, clinical treatment, and training to parents, agencies, schools, mental health workers, social workers, judges, and attorneys.

Website: http://www.kinnect.org/training.html #fact

CASE: The Center for Adoption Support and Education, Inc., 4000 Blackburn Ln., Suite 260, Burtonsville, MD 20866

Telephone: (301) 476-8525; Fax: (301) 476-8526; e-mail: aseadopt@adoptionsupport.org

Website: http://www.adoption support.org

Provides postadoption counseling and educational services to families, educators, child welfare staff, and mental health providers in the Metropolitan Washington, DC area. Provides national training and consultation that integrates theory, strategies, and innovative models. Resources include W.I.S.E. UP Powerbook to assist children to stand up against adoption bias.

Adoptees' Liberty Movement Association (ALMA), PO Box 85, Denville, NJ 07834

Telephone: (973) 586-1358; Fax: (973) 586-1358; e-mail: MAnderson@almasociety.org

Website: http://www.almasociety.org

Adoptees' Liberty Movement Association (ALMA), a membership organization, is an adoption reunion registry. ALMA advocates for the right of adopted persons to know the truth of their origin.

Concerned United Birthparents (CUB), PO Box 230457, Encinitas, CA 92150-3475

Toll-Free: (800) 822-2777; e-mail: info@CUBirthparents.org

Website: http://www.cubirthparents.org

CUB's mission is to provide support to birthparents who have relinquished a child to adoption, to provide resources to help prevent unnecessary family separations, to educate the public about the lifelong effects on all who are touched by adoption, and to advocate for fair and ethical adoption laws, policies, and practices.

Adoption Agencies Specializing in Open Adoption

Buckner Adoption and Maternity Services, 5200 S. Buckner Blvd.,Dallas, TX 75227

Telephone: (214) 319-3426 Fax: (214) 319-3470

www.buckneradoption.org

Buckner is the largest faith-based, non-profit family service agency in the country; offering services to adoptive parents, birth parents and children. Offers domestic infant, foster to adoption, CPS adoption, and comprehensive lifelong services before, during, and after placement. Specializes in an ethical, child-centered approach to developing relationships between birth and adoptive parents.

Open Adoption & Family Services, 5200 SW Macadam Avenue, Suite 250, Portland, Oregon 97201

Telephone: (503) 226-4870 Fax (503) 226-4891

Website: www.openadopt.org

Catholic Charities, 1000 Hastings, Traverse City, MI 49686

Telephone: (231)947-8110

E-mail: Catholichumanservice.com

Tracing its commitment to open adoption back to 1980, Catholic Human Services has served as one of the nation's foremost proponents of openness. The agency hosted the first national conference centering on open adoption in 1982, and went on to hold eight additional conferences. The staff has provided training in 26 states and provinces.

Contact Information for Practitioners Cited in
Making Room in Our hearts

Cooperative Adoption, Ellen Roseman Curtis, 54 Wellington Avenue, San Anselmo, CA 94960

Telephone: (415) 453-0902; Fax: (415) 455-9449; e-mail: ellen@coopadopt.com

Facilitates independent and agency adoptions. Education and preparation for developing open relationships. Ellen Roseman has served as the Southwest Regional Chair of the American Adoption Congress; she is on the board of the Northern California Chapter of Resolve, and has been active in adoption legislation.

Carol L. Demuth, LCSW, PO Box 460024, Garland, TX 75046-0024

Telephone: (972) 414-3639; e-mail: cldemuth@yahoo.com

Carol Demuth works with Buckner Adoption and Maternity Services, and maintains a private practice providing counseling, education, and mediation services to those affected by infertility, child loss, adoption, and assisted reproduction. She is available as a trainer in the fields of infertility and adoption. Ms. Demuth is a reunited adoptee, and has authored *Courageous Blessing: Adoptive Parents and the Search; Considerations in Adopting Beyond Infancy*, and is the creator of the video *Talking with Your Child about Adoption*.

Patricia Martinez Dorner, MA, LPC, LMFT Adoption Counseling and Search, 206 Lochaven Lane, San Antonio, TX

Telephone and Fax (210) 341-2070; e-mail: pdorner@satx.rr.com

Patricia Martinez Dorner is the author of *How to Open an Adoption: A Guide For Parents and Birthparents of Minors; ADOPTION SEARCH: An Ethical Guide for Professionals; Talking to Your Child about Adoption; ADOPCION: hablando con tu hijo*; and coauthor of *Children of Open Adoption*. Ms. Dorner's adoption focused practice includes counseling, search assistance, and the opening of adoptions involving minors. In 1999, she was awarded the Baran Pannor Award for Outstanding Contributions in Open Adoption.

James Gritter, MSW, 8865 Crockett, Williamsburg, MI 49690

Telephone: (231) 947-8110; e-mail: Jimgrit@aol.com

Jim Gritter is the editor of *Adoption Without Fear* and author of *The Spirit of Open Adoption, Lifegivers: Framing the Birthparent Experience in Adoption*, and (forthcoming) *Adoptive Hospitality*. Designated a "Social Work Pioneer" by the NASW, he is available for training on child-centered open adoption.

Mary Martin Mason, 4012 Lynn Avenue, Edina MN 55416

Telephone: (952) 926-2848; e-mail: mmason@mnadopt.org

Ms. Mason is a nationally recognized author and trainer with a specialty in open adoption; Adoption Information Coordinator for Minnesota Adoption Support and Preservation (MN ASAP); Legislative Chair for American Adoption Congress; Board Member of Gift of Adoption Foundation; Author of *Out of the Shadows: Birthfathers' Stories, Designing Rituals in Adoption*, and *The Miracle Seekers*, as well as numerous nationally published articles about adoption.

Center For Family Connections, Dr. Joyce Maguire Pavao, CEO and Founder, 350 Cambridge Street, Cambridge, MA 02141

Telephone: (617) 547-0909; Fax: (617) 497 5952

Website: http://www.kinnect.org

Dr. Pavao is the author of the book *The Family of Adoption*, and numerous articles on the normative crisis in the development of the adoptive family. She is an internationally recognized expert who is available for education, consultation, clinical treatment, and training for parents, agencies, schools, mental health workers, social workers, judges, and attorneys. She has received many honors and awards, including the North American Council for Adoptable Children for *Adoption Activist* and *Child Advocate of the Year*, and the Baran/Pannor Award for *Excellence in Open Adoption*.

Insight: Open Adoption Resources and Support, Brenda Romanchik, MSW, Founder and director. 721 Hawthorne, Royal Oak, MI 48067

Telephone/Fax: (248) 543-0997; Expectant parent/birthparent resource line: (877) 879-0669; e-mail: brenr@openadoptioninsight.org

Website http://www.openadoptioninsight.org

Ms. Romanchik is dedicated to educating professionals, triad members, and the public about open adoption. Offers training programs to hospital personnel, adoption professionals, and crisis pregnancy centers. Author of *Being a Birthparent: Fnding Our Place*; *Birthparent Grief, and Your rights and Responsibilities*. Sponsors The Lifegiver's Festival, a conference for birthparents on open adoptions, and Shared Connections, a conference for birth mothers and adoptive mothers.

Kinship Center, Sharon Roszia M.S., 1504 Brookhollow Drive, Suite 118, Santa Ana, CA 92705

Telephone (714) 979-2365; e-mail: sroszia@kinshipcenter.org

Ms. Roszia is the Program Manager of The Kinship Center, where she has pioneered open adoption practice. The coauthor, (with Lois Melina) of *The Open Adoption Experience, Creating Kinship* (with Baran and Coleman), and *Cooperative Adoption: The Official Handbook*, with Rillera. Her articles and training on the seven core issues of adoption has widely influenced adoption practice and understanding. She is available as a trainer and consultant for all adoption related issues.

Magazines, Newsletters, and Adoption Books

Adoptive Families Magazine, Editorial and Advertising Offices, 39 West 37th Street, 15th Floor, New York, NY 10018

Telephone: (646) 366-0830; Fax: (646) 366-0842; Subscription Customer Service: 800-372-3300; e-mail: letters@adoptivefamilies.com

FAIR: Families Adopting in Response; (FAIR), PO Box 51436, Palo Alto, CA 94303

Telephone (650) 856-3513; e-mail: info@fairfamilies.org

Available from FAIR: *Adoption and the Schools: Resources for Parents and Teach*ers; Everything parents and teachers need to support adopted children in school.

Family Voices: Adoption Support and Preservation Newsletter **MN ASAP FAMILY Voices*** is published quarterly by MN ASAP, a collaboration of the Minnesota Adoption Resource Network (MARN) and the North American Council on Adoptable Children (NACAC). Contact: Mary Martin Mason at Telephone: (612) 798-4033 or (877) 966-2727.

Insight: Open Adoption Resources and Support, Brenda Romanchik, MSW. 721 Hawthorne, Royal Oak, MI 48067

Telephone: (248) 543-0997; e-mail: brenr@openadoption insight.org

Publishes guidebooks for birth parents: *Birth Parent Grief; Your Rights and Responsibilities*; *Being a Birthparent, Finding our Place.*

Perspectives Press, PO Box 90318, Indianapolis, IN 46290-0318;

Telephone: (317) 872-3055; e-mail: info@perspectivespress.com

Website:www.perspectivespress.com

Publishes award-winning books on infertility, adoption, reproductive health, and child welfare issues. Provides workshops for consumers and for medical, mental health, and counseling professionals on infertility, alternative family building, and adoption.

Tapestry Books, PO Box 6448, Hillsborough NJ 08844

Telephone: (800) 765-2367 (U.S. only) or (908) 359-8198; Fax: (908) 359-6450; e-mail: owner@tapestrybooks.com

Website: http://www.tapestrybooks.com

Tapestry Books specializes in adoption, infertility, and parenting books. Current catalog has over 200 books with brief descriptions of each.

Open Adoption Tools

Open Adoption & Family Services, 5200 SW Macadam Avenue, Suite 250, Portland, Oregon 97201

Telephone: (503) 226-4870; Fax: (503) 226-4891; e-mail: information@openadopt.org

Website: http://www.openadopt.org

Please seek written permission from Open Adoption & Family Services prior to making multiple photocopies.

Adoption Myths and Facts for Birth Fathers

Myth: There is no role for me in the adoption planning process. It is designed to meet only the needs of the birth mother.

Fact: Birth fathers are very important in the adoption planning process. Your needs and wishes will be respected and discussed in order to create a plan that is inclusive of all parties. You are entitled to free individual counseling, just as the birth mother is, and are encouraged to take advantage of this service.

Myth: Real men keep their children. Only deadbeat dads choose adoption.

Fact: A responsible father ensures that all of his child's social, emotional, and financial needs are met by whatever means necessary. Deciding that adoption best meets a child's needs is not shameful; it is an honorable, difficult, and loving choice.

Myth: My child will hate me if I plan an adoption and will think I abandoned him or her.

Fact: Adoption is not, in any way, abandonment. By being involved in an open adoption plan and committing to an ongoing relationship with the child and the adoptive family, you are taking an active and important role in ensuring the well-being of your child. When children have little or no contact with their biological fathers, they tend to develop unrealistically strong feelings of love or hate for them, casting birth fathers as heroes or villains. The ongoing contact afforded by open adoption allows birth fathers to develop realistic and balanced relationships with their children.

Myth: Birthfathers don't care what happens to their children.

Fact: We know from experience that birth fathers deeply love their children. But they often feel their role in adoption is nonexistent, or undefined at best. The open adoption process welcomes you and helps you identify ways to stay involved in your child's life and to actively demonstrate your care and concern.

Myth: Children of open adoption don't care about and need their birth fathers as much as they do their birth mothers.

Fact: Adoptive children want and deserve to know their birth fathers just as much as their birth mothers. Both birth parents provide critical keys to a child's emotional security and his or her genetic history.

Myth: I should be ashamed of choosing not to parent. My friends and family will think less of me if they find out I planned an adoption.

Fact: Many people are unfamiliar with open adoption. As you educate your friends and family about the process, and actively demonstrate your ongoing connection to your child, they will become more familiar with open adoption and, consequently, more supportive.

http://www.openadopt.org

Toward an Ethical and Values-Based Adoption Practice

Adoption professionals can use the following as a starting point for discussion and evaluation of the values and practices in their own programs.

Values Based Open Adoption—A Statement of Beliefs

This Statement of Beliefs is the work of Jim Gritter at Catholic Human Services in Michigan with the input of the participants at the National Open Adoption Conferences he managed during the 1980s and 1990s. This version was presented at the Fifth National Conference on Open Adoption, in 1995. This copy is reprinted here with Mr. Gritter's permission. If you would like to send any comments or questions to Jim Gritter his e-mail is jimgrit@aol.com

1. We understand open adoption to be a transfer of parental responsibilities that preserves the relationship between birthparents and the child they entrusted to the family they painstakingly selected. It necessarily includes a full disclosure of identifying information and features a commitment to lifelong relatedness.
2. We believe that every form of adoption must center on meeting the needs of the adoptee. We believe that children are best served by preserving their connection to their family of origin.
3. We assert that there is a tragic dimension to adoption. Every participant in adoption experiences pain and loss. Any significant description of the adoption experience must recognize the theme of loss.
4. We believe the first effort in working with pregnant families must be to preserve that family.
5. We are committed to protecting the rights of birthfathers. We recognize that they are important in the lives of their children and seek their full participation in the open adoption experience.
6. We believe birth families require at least fourteen days following the birth of the child to consider their options before legally committing themselves to an adoption plan. We will respect a birthfamily's sense of pace.
7. We recognize a professional obligation to assist clients to reach fully informed decisions. We will defend families facing the challenges of untimely pregnancy from premature feelings of obligation, and will defend their opportunity to change course in timely fashion.
8. We recognize that geographic distance makes open adoption more difficult to plan, implement, and sustain. Professionals are obliged to alert clients to reliable resources that may be more conveniently located.
9. We recognize that adoption is a lifelong experience and that adoption organizations must remain a resource to our clients through the years.
10. We believe adoption services must not yield personal or organizational profit.
11. We will operate our program with fiscal integrity and openness. We will work to keep our fees affordable so participation in our program does not require financial prosperity.
12. We recognize an obligation to share significant results, positive and negative, with other professionals in the field and also with the wider public.
13. We recognize that the spirit of candor needs to be applied to adoptions from the past. We actively support open records and the right of adoptive persons to their original name.
14. We believe adoption programs ought be evaluated in terms of quality, not quantity.
15. We believe that efforts to promote particular programs must never offend the general public's sense of propriety. We believe the commercialization of adoption diminishes the dignity of children.
16. We believe the vitality of the institution of adoption is directly linked to its commitment to candor. We approach every adoption with the presumption it will be open. Any departure from candor is considered extraordinary and requires documented justification.
17. We believe the spirit of openness and candor begins with the professional. It is his or her responsibility to create a climate in which overall honesty is encouraged and reinforced.

18. We believe the most promising context for the delivery of ethical adoption services is the nonprofit agency. We acknowledge that our organizations often fall short of our ideals. To live up to their potential, agencies must relentlessly root out inconsistencies and self-serving practices.

19. We recognize that we are powerful because we hold significant information. We recognize our responsibility to pass this power to our clients throughout the adoptive process by emphasizing the educational features of our program.

20. We recognize that integrity requires consistency in our beliefs and actions. We will select our affiliations carefully, supporting organizations whose purposes and practices are consistent with ours, and working to reeducate organizations whose practices are in direct opposition to our beliefs.

21. We believe that dynamic adoptive practice engenders a spirit of community. We strive to provide adoption cultures in which financial and emotional risks are shared. There should be no monetary connection between adoptive parents and birthparents.

22. We believe adoptions of quality are adaptable. Every adoption will be a unique expression of the original and continuing creativity of its participants.

23. We believe the practice of open adoption is dynamic and continually evolving. We are receptive to responsible innovation.

References

Brodzinsky, D. (Mar. 2002) *Addressing issues of origin respectfully.* Presentation at Pact's 5th Annual Spring Training.

Brodzinsky, D. (April 2004) *The relationship with birth parents when there is no contact.* Presentation at Pact's 7th Annual Spring Training.

Brodzinsky, D., Schecter, M., & Marantz Hening, R. (1992). *Being adopted: The lifelong search for self.* New York, NY: Doubleday.

Carp, W. (1998). *Family matters: Secrecy and disclosure in the history of adoption.* Cambridge, MA: Harvard University Press.

Cox, S. Soon-Keum (Oct. 2005). *Finding home: Fifty years of international adoptions.* American Radio Works of American Public Media

Dorner, P. M., Silber, K. (1989). *Children of open adoption.* San Antonio, TX. Corona Press

Dorner, P. M. (1997). How to open an adoption. Royal Oak, MI: R-Square Press.

Freundlich, M. (Summer, Fall 1998) Clinical Mediation: Preventing and resolving adoption disputes, Part I & II. *Decree: Newsletter of American Adoption Congress.*

Gritter, J. (2004). *Adoptive parent's attitudes towards birth parents.* Presentation at PACT's 7th Annual Spring Training.

Gritter, J. (2000). *Life givers: Framing the birth parent experience in open adoption.* Washington, DC: CWLA Press.

Gritter, J. (1997). *The spirit of open adoption.* Washington, DC CWLA Press.

Grotevant, H., & McRoy, R. (1998). *Openness in adoption: Exploring family connections.* Thousand Oaks, CA: Sage Publications.

Johnson, P. I. (1992). *Adopting after infertility.* Indianapolis, IN: Perspectives Press.

Kirk, R. (1983). *Shared fate.* Brentwood, BC: Ben-Simon.

Lifton, B. J. (1994). *Journey of the adopted self: A quest for wholeness.* New York: Basic Books.

Martin, A. M. (2005). *A dog's life: The autobiography of a stray.* New York: Scholastic.

Mason, M. M. (1995). *Out of the shadows:* Birthfathers'*stories.* O.J. Howard Publishing: Edina, MN.

Melina, L. (Jan.1998). *Adoption issues being revealed, iceberg metaphor; Chosen vs. "unchosen".* Keynote and workshop presentation at Northern California Chapter of Resolve Adoption Symposium.

Melina, L., & Rosza, S. K. (1993). *The open adoption experience.* New York: Harper Perennial.

McRoy, R. (July 2002) *Longitudinal outcomes of openness in adoption: implications for birthmothers, adoptive parents and adopted cihldren.* Presentation at Kinship's Center's Adoption Education Institute.

Mock Springer M. (2006, Winter Vol.7 p. 58-64). From afar. *Brain, Child: The Magazine for Thinking Mothers*

Pavao, J. M. (1998). *The family of adoption.* Boston, MA: Beacon.

Pertman, A. (2000). *The adoption nation.* New York: Basic Books.

Romanchik, B. (1999). *Being a birth parent, finding our place.* Royal Oak, MI: R-Squared Press.

Romer, S. (Mar. 2004). *Adoption agreements.* Presentation at the Northern California Resolve Adoption Symposium.

Silber, K., & Dorner, P. M. (1989). *Children of open adoption.* San Antonio, TX: Corona.

Sorosky, A., Baran, A., & Pannor, R. (1989). *The adoption triangle: Sealed or open records: How they affect adoptees, birth parents, and adoptive parents.* San Antonio, TX: Corona.

Steinberg, G., & Hall, B. (2000). *Inside transracial adoption.* Indianapolis, IN: Perspectives Press.

Acknowledgments

I want to thank the birth and adoptive family members from across the country who responded to the questionnaires or e-mail inquiries and generously shared intimate stories about their lives and relationships. My own heart was opened as I listened to their joys and challenges, and above all, their commitment to their children. Many of those who responded were not profiled here, but their carefully considered reflections informed the writing of this book. All of these stories confirmed that openness begins when you are able to "make room in your hearts" for an inclusive idea of family. Many of these family members could not have found their way to me if it were not for the generous willingness of Patricia Martinez Dorner to email all her contacts and invite them to respond to the questionnaire. Others who assisted with names and contacts were Mary Martin Mason, James Gritter, and Ellen Roseman. I could not have done this without your assistance.

I am grateful for the generosity, experience, and wisdom of the following open adoption experts who participated in interviews with me either in person or via telephone: Kathleen Cleary, Executive Director, Consortium for Children; Carol Demuth, counselor and educator, Buckner Adoption and Maternity Services; Patricia Martinez Dorner, Adoption educator, counselor and author; Adela Jones, director Domestic Adoptions, Buckner Adoption and Maternity Services; Gloria King, executive director, Black Adoption Placement and Research Center; Shari Levine, director, Open Adoption and Family Services; Carolyn Mitchell, former trainer and social worker for Kinship Center; Susan Quash-Mah, Teamwork For Children; Cheryl Roberts, social work supervisor, Lilliput Adoptions; Brenda Romanchik, Director, Insight, Open Adoption Resources and Support; Tom Rutherford, former program director, Consortium for Children.

I deeply appreciate those who took precious time from their demanding schedules to read this manuscript: Leslie Foge, James Gritter, Beth Hall, Susan Ito, Joyce Maguire Pavao, Adam Pertman, Sharon Roszia, Brenda Romanchik, Jean Strauss, and Ada White. Your willingness to consider or write recommendations for this book made it feel blessed by many who have taught me so much about adoption. I am deeply thankful to each of you. Leslie Foge provided me with much needed encouragement during the arduous search for a publisher, in addition to feedback and support during a critical time in the process. I also want to thank those reviewers, both known and unknown, who provided excellent and constructive feedback to me via Rutgers University Press and Routledge.

I am fortunate to have found a publisher in George Zimmar at Routledge, who saw the need for this book in both the academic arena and in the adoption community. I deeply appreciate that he has been receptive to my hopes and ideas for the intimate look and feel of this book. Dana Bliss, an associate editor, guided me through the publishing process with patience and clarity, and endured the many straggling pieces of information that remained at loose ends until the very end. I received excellent editing from a colleague, Sheila Madden, and sound advice during the contract process from Victoria Shoemaker, a Bay Area agent.

My valued friend, Linda Williams, was supportive throughout by consistently inquiring about the book's progress. Always willing to hear about the latest obstacle, she helped me think through it by her insightful and supportive questions. During the almost three years that I tried to carve out time to work on this project, many of my friends saw less of me and received far fewer phone calls and e-mails. I look forward to renewing our friendships.

Last and certainly not least, I want to thank my husband, partner, and best buddy, Steve Thomasberger, for putting up with me. He endured far too many bouts of a first-time author who kept anxiously raising her voice: "How am I going to be able to finish this book if I don't get more time?" Thank goodness that he is not only patient and forgiving, but also such a good cook!! If it were not for the magic that brought my daughter to me, I would not have had the need to write this book. A commitment to her moved us toward openness, and has guided me to enrich the adoption community's understanding of the need to make room in our hearts in order to keep family ties.

Index

Loss feelings
    by birth parents, 27–28
    by child, 8
    resources for, 158
    strengthening effects of, 14
Loyalty, 33

M

Magazines, 162–163
Mediation, 75–76, 124, 143
Melina, Lois, 12–14, 62, 121
Misunderstandings, 128
Mitchell, Carolyn, 74–75
Mock, Melanie Springer, 146
Mother, *See* Adoptive parents; Birth mother
Multicultural model, 145
Multiple birth families, 100–102
Multiracial family, 92–97

N

Nesler, Joey, 14
Newsletters, 162–163

O

Open adoption
    adoptive parents in, 21–22, 24, 30–31,
        41–42, 59–61, 76, 80–82, 93–96,
        118, 147–148
    advocates for, 10–11
    benefits of, 2–3, 8, 31, 48, 154
    between best friends, 110–112
    birth father's inclusion in, 139–140
    birth mothers in, 17–20, 27, 36–38,
        50–54, 131, 150–151, 153
    birth parents in, 24, 58, 84, 86
    boundaries in, 118–122
    case studies of, 17–22, 35–39, 129–131
    child-centered
        description of, 16–17
        education, 135–140, 143
        recommendations for, 143–144
    children in, 20–21, 24, 38–39, 96–97
    closed adoption and, in same family,
        107–110
    contributing factors for, 10
    counseling about, 138–139
    difficulties in, 5, 113
    education about, 135
    foundation building for, 6
    fully, 17, 146
    openness vs., 114, 153
    principles of, 30

process vs. structure in, 114–115
professionals used in, 87–89
proponents of, 2
recommendations for, 143–144
research about, 23–24
resources about, 157
secrets in, 102–107
sense of self affected by, 48, 154
success of, 128
support for, 135
traits helpful for, 113–114
transracial adoption, 89–92
Open Adoption Experience, The, 23, 25
Openness
    accountability issues, 101
    benefits of, 83
    boundary setting and, 121
    case studies of, 147–151
    challenges associated with, 96, 99
    choosing of, 136
    concerns about
        by adoptive parents, 118
        by birth parents, 84–85, 115, 118
        claiming of child as one's own, 31–32,
            83
        confusion by child, 33–34
        contact, 28–30
        description of, 83–85
        "real" parents, 32–33, 44
    contributing factors for, 10
    evolving nature of, 54
    family building through, 146–147
    genuineness in, 114
    grandparents' views on, 49
    importance of dialogue for, 34–35
    in international adoptions, 68–72, 146
    open adoption vs., 114, 153
    as an opportunity, 31
    perspectives on, 153
    in public adoption system, 75–77
    success of, 128
    support for, 135
    transracial adoption and, 63–64
Organizations, 158–160
Origins
    child's search for, 83
    search for, 15

P

Pact, 1, 63–64
Pannor, Rueben, 2–3, 10
Parent(s)
    adoptive, *See* Adoptive parents

Printed by Publishers' Graphics Kentucky